Joan Fuster
Aphorisms

CATALAN STUDIES
IN CULTURE AND LINGUISTICS

Edited by
Antonio Cortijo Ocaña

VOLUME 9

PETER LANG

Berlin - Bruxelles - Chennai - Lausanne - New York - Oxford

Joan Fuster

Aphorisms

Translated into English by Antonio Cortijo-Rodgers
Studies by Antonio Cortijo-Rodgers and Vicent Salvador

Berlin · Bruxelles · Chennai · Lausanne · New York · Oxford

Library of Congress Cataloging-in-Publication
A CIP record for this book has been applied for at the Library of Congress.

Bibliographic information published by the Deutsche Nationalbibliothek
The Deutsche Nationalbibliothek lists this publication in the Deutsche Nationalbibliografie; detailed bibliographic data is available on the Internet at http://dnb.d-nb.de.

This work has been edited and translated with the support of the Institut Ramon Llull The resulting literary, cultural, linguistic and translatological study was carried out by the Institut Superior d'Investigació Cooperativa IVITRA [ISIC-IVITRA] (Programa per a la Constitució i Acreditació d'Instituts Superiors d'Investigació Cooperativa d'Excel·lència de la Generalitat Valenciana, Ref. ISIC/012/042), attached to the Dept. of Catalan Philology of the Universitat d'Alacant [UA], and within the frame of the following research projects and institutions: MICINUN, Ref. PID2021-128381NB-I00; Institució Alfons el Magnànim; Observatori multilingüe de la variació lingüística-OMVALING (Programa Prometeu de la Generalitat Valenciana Prometeu per a grups de recerca d'excel.lència, RefPROMETEO/2023/6); IEC; Grup d'Investigació VIGROB-125 de la UA; and Seu Universitària de la Nucia [UA]). Special thanks to Prof. Dr. Dr. Vicent Martines because he has made possible the management of this edition

ISSN 2627-468X
ISBN 978-3-631-92643-7 (Print)
E-ISBN 978-3-631-92685-7 (E-PDF)
E-ISBN 978-3-631-92686-4 (EPUB)
DOI 10.3726/b22354

© 2024 Peter Lang Group AG, Lausanne
Published by Peter Lang GmbH, Berlin, Germany

info@peterlang.com – www.peterlang.com

All rights reserved.

All parts of this publication are protected by copyright.
Any utilization outside the strict limits of the copyright law, without the permission of the publisher, is forbidden and liable to prosecution. This applies in particular to reproductions, translations, microfilming, and storage and processing in electronic retrieval systems.

Contents

Fuster's *Aforisms* and the Tradition of Ἀφορισμός/Aphorismi 7
   Proverbs, Adages, and Emblems 13
   Montaigne and the *Essai* 16
   Friedrich Nietzsche 18
   Ramón Gómez de la Serna 19
   Finally, Fuster 20

Fuster and Aphorisms 21

APHORISMS 31

Final Judgments 31
   Prejudices 31
   Knowing What I am Talking About 31
   Ethics for a Stranger 39
   Works and Days 47
   For One, For Many 55
   General Absolution and Plenary Indulgence 63

Indecent Proposals 65
   Initial Caution 65
   Randomly Observed 65
   Ideas for Family Children 69
   Personal Experience 72
   Philosophy and Letters 76
   The Art of Giving Rabbits 80
   They Call It «SOCIETY» 83

I Am Temporarily Closing the Parenthesis 88
Few Words 89
About Other Final Judgments 97
    I 97
    II 98
    III 100
    IV 101
    V 102
    VI 103

Antonio Cortijo-Rodgers

(University of California)

Fuster's *Aforisms* and the Tradition of Ἀφορισμός/Aphorismi

Joan Fuster offers us in *Poetry, aphorisms, Diary, Vignettes and Drawings* a collection of maxims, apothegms, and aphorisms that constitute a series of philosophical reflections on a variety of topics. The author purposely rejects a fully developed narrative style as well as a more methodical and comprehensive approach to the presentation of his ideas. Instead, he chooses the seemingly innocuous and more humble style of the laconic and brief note to offer us what could be termed his inconsequential musings on life. But Fuster is not alone in this way of approaching the essay and the philosophical genre. In fact, he belongs to a long list of philosophers who have prioritized this form and style in their writings, from the classical Greek and Roman period, to more contemporary examples.

The word ἀφορισμός derives from the verb ἀφορίζω, 'to mark off', 'to divide', 'to distinguish'. In turn, the word is a composite of the prefix ἀπό-, 'from', and the verb ὁρίζω, 'to define', 'to bound'. The Oxford Dictionary defines an aphorism as "a pithy observation that contains a general truth, such as, 'if it ain't broke, don't fix it'". It can also be "a concise statement of a scientific principle, typically by an ancient classical author." Some synonyms are "sayings", "maxims", "axioms", "adages", "precepts", "epigrams", "dictums", "gnomes", "proverbs", or "apothegms", among others. Aphorisms state principles, general truths or sentiments in a dazzling, terse way. Joan Fuster is fascinated by this genre, as proven by the fact that before *Poetry, Aphorisms, Diary, Vignettes and Drawings* he had published another book of aphorisms entitled *Advice, Proverbs, Impertinences*. His own definition and conceptualization of an *aphorism* is included in the former title as follows:

> These notes, brief and sometimes epigrammatic, are a continuation of the book *Consells, proverbis i insolències* that I published in 1968. I have many more in the drawer. I have not made a hasty selection, and I would not want anybody to interpret this one as particularly significant. To write an aphorism is usually a slow process, costly in rectifications, perplex in ratifications, responsible for the nuances of some word or other. It is an archaic and not very fashionable «literary genre», although they fascinate me. They are one more «paper hat», which only aspires to have the interests of a personal «point of view» in mind. Contradictory? Perhaps, perhaps not. And I do not care.

Of particular relevance is Fuster's statement that these laconic, concise, pithy, memorable, and epigrammatic notes require a long period of reflection. The author's philosophical musings result in concentrated expressions of a contradictory or paradoxical nature, frequently skeptical and with an acerbic humor. In fact, it is this paradoxical nature which appealed to classical philosophers. Fuster's work has a deep rooting in classical humanism which was, as critics have pointed out, close in spirit to the moralists and French reformers of the 16th and 17th centuries (from Quevedo and Montaigne to the French encyclopedists).

Aphorisms are a substantial part of the style of several classical thinkers. The name, which means *distinction* or *definition*, was first used by Hippocrates (c. 460 BC-c. 370 BC) in his book *Aphorisms* (Ἀφορισμοί; *Aphorismi*) to refer to his sententious statements on physical science and medicine concerning the symptoms and diagnoses of disease and the art of healing and medicine. Hippocrates is reputed to have imitated this style in his treatises from Heraclitus. The famous first sentence of Hippocrates's book states:

Ὁ βίος βραχύς, ἡ δὲ τέχνη μακρή, ὁ δὲ καιρὸς ὀξύς, ἡ δὲ πεῖρα σφαλερή, ἡ δὲ κρίσις χαλεπή. Δεῖ δὲ οὐ μόνον ἑωυτὸν παρέχειν τὰ δέοντα ποιεῦντα, ἀλλὰ καὶ τὸν νοσέοντα, καὶ τοὺς παρεόντας, καὶ τὰ ἔξωθεν. (1.1)

[Life is short, and art long; the crisis fleeting; experience perilous, and decision difficult. The physician must not only be prepared to do what is right himself, but also to make the patient, the attendants, and externals cooperate.] (1.1) (my translation)

The aphoristic tradition also permeated the writings of other classical Greek authors, namely pre-Socratic philosophers. Among those mentioned by tradition as writers of pithy sentences and founders of an aphoristic style are Solon (c. 640 – c. 556 BC) and Heraclitus from Ephesus (fl. c. 500 BC), both of whom predated Hippocrates. Most of the *sayings* of classical philosophers have been preserved to us in an aphoristic format thanks to Diogenes Laertius's *Lives and Opinions of the Eminent Philosophers* (Βίοι καὶ γνῶμαι τῶν ἐν φιλοσοφίᾳ εὐδοκιμησάντων; *Vitae philosophorum*; *Liber de vita et moribus philosophorum*) (fl. 3rd AD), which uses previous work by Favorinus and Diocles of Magnesia, among several others.

Solon was the author of the famous aphorism *nothing too much* (μηδὲν ἄγαν; nihil nimis). Heraclitus developed a philosophy expressed in an epigrammatic and oracular language whose exact meaning and interpretation remain obscure and controversial, "as is the inference often drawn from this theory that in the world as Heraclitus conceives it contradictory propositions must be true" (Graham). Among his most famous aphorisms, we could mention the following: "Everything flows, nothing remains" (πάντα χωρεῖ καὶ οὐδὲν μένει); "everything is in flux" (πάντα ῥεῖ); and especially "You could never step in the same river twice", for it's not the same river (δὶς ἐς τὸν αὐτὸν ποταμὸν οὐκ ἂν ἐμβαίης). Parmenides (fl. 475 BC), who is reputed to be the founder of ontology and metaphysics, set out to refute Heraclitus's tenets, and he did so in his *On Nature*, most of which has survived and is composed to a great extent of aphoristic statements such as "whatever is is, and what is not cannot be". A variation on the aphoristic form is represented by the style of the paradoxes of one of Parmenides's followers, Zenon of Elea (ca. 495 – ca. 430 BC), who is credited with the invention of dialectic. Diogenes the Cynic (ca. 404 – ca. 323 BC), according to Diogenes Laertius, was a disciple of Antisthenes, a student of Socrates. He defended a love of virtue and indifference to wealth. He also believed that virtue should be predicated by actions and not theories, and devoted his life of extreme poverty to criticize with his behaviour and stunts the social values and institutions of a corrupt society. He was considered of a dog-like nature because of his shamelessness, his staunch defence of philosophical truth, his distinguishing instinctively between friend and foe, and his recognizing those not suited to philosophy and barking at them. Some of his axioms include "If I lack awareness, then why should I care what happens to me when I am dead?"; "Humans have complicated every simple gift of the gods", and "I am a citizen of the world".

Two philosophical doctrines and the authors that belong to them are particularly associated with the writing of axioms and aphorisms: Epicureanism and Stoicism. Epicurus (341–270 BC), an ardent opposer of Platonism, taught that people should behave morally, and that through knowledge learned by experience and not reason they should seek ataraxia. Ataraxia, 'untroubledness', is a state in which a person is free from pain or suffering, and can be obtained by following the *tetrapharmakos*: don't fear god, don't worry about death, what is good is easy to get, what is terrible is easy to endure. Epicurus's doctrine has been preserved to us through a variety of writings, in particular the collection of maxims included in Diogenes Laertius's *Lives and*

Opinions of the Eminent Philosophers that come directly from Epicurus's Κύριαι Δόξαι (*Principal Doctrines*). Epicureanism can be summarized by the following aphorism preserved as a frequent epitaph found in many ancient Roman tombstones: *Non fui, fui, non sum, non curo* ("I was not, I was, I am not, I do not care").

Among the Stoics, aphorisms and apothegms were greatly appreciated. A special place is reserved for Seneca (Lucius Annaeus Seneca the Younger, ca. 4 BC – 65 AD) who enjoyed great fame during the Middle Ages and the Renaissance, partly due to his acceptance by Christian authorities and his association with St Paul. His books on ethics were widely disseminated offering practical advice and theoretical discussions in the form of maxims and aphorisms. Works like *De providentia, De ira, De vita beata, De beneficiis, De otio, De tranquillitate animi, De consolatione* and especially his *Epistulae morales ad Lucilium* emphasize striving to reach ethical perfection through the curtailment of destructive passions and the cultivation of friendship, clemency, moderation, and acceptance of diversity. His influence was pervasive and his work inspired collections of maxims, such as the *Formula vitae honestae* attributed to St. Martin of Braga (ca. 580), and Petrarch's famous *De remediis utriusque Fortunae* (14th c.). Seneca's philosophy can be summarized through a series of maxims: "Fallaces sunt rerum species" (The appearances of things are deceptive); "Fata volentem ducunt, nolentem trahunt" (Destiny carries the willing man, and drags the unwilling"); "Errare humanum est, perseverare diabolicum" (To err is human, to persevere in it, is diabolical); "Animum debes mutare non caelum" (You should change your attitude, not your sky); "Aequat omnes cinis" (Ashes make everybody equal); "Divitiae bonum non sunt" (Material wealth is not the one good). A great follower of Seneca, Montaigne, was often called the "French Seneca".

Emperor Marcus Aurelius (121 – 180 AD) is also one of the best-known references for Stoic doctrine, together with Seneca. Educated in Greek and Latin letters by Herodes Atticus and Marcus Cornelius Fronto, Marcus Aurelius composed the 12 books of his *Meditations* (Τὰ εἰς ἑαυτόν). This book is composed of fragmentary and epigrammatic philosophical reflections intended only for himself as a way to relieve the tensions of his military campaigns. *Meditations* advocates the basic tenets of Stoicism, such as the avoidance of indulgence, finding one's place in the universe ("The universe is transformation; our life is what our thoughts make it"), accepting that everything comes from nature and shall return to it ("All things from eternity are of like forms and come round in a circle"), following rationality and clear-mindedness ("Whatever this is that I am, it is a little flesh and breath, and the ruling part"), and maintaining strong ethical principles: "And thou wilt give thyself relief, if thou doest every act of thy life as if it were the last". He emphasizes the need for acceptance of nature as the guiding human principle, "Whatever may happen to you was prepared for you from all eternity; and the implication of causes was from eternity spinning the thread of your being".

Aphorisms with philosophical content can also be found in Greek and Latin literature in almost all literary genres. Pre-Socratic philosophers, playwrights, Plato, Aristotle, Cicero, and early Christian writers are a good source of numerous axioms, proverbs, and formulae that reflect their wide use and dissemination in the classical period. In addition, many of these maxims were gathered in the form of *florilegia* or anthologies and were used throughout the Middle Ages for educational purposes. During the Middle Ages, aphoristic literature became one of the preferred ways to teach students the Latin language as well as moral principles. Among the many books that belong to this genre, perhaps none was more popular than the *Disticha Catonis* (*Distichs of Cato*), used in conjunction with Aesop's *Fabulae* in the initial stages of a student's curriculum. The *Disticha* became part of the canon of medieval *auctoritates* and is composed of simple distichs of moral maxims. As Alvar Núño and Borsari state, "the Benedictine monk Conrad of Hirsau (12th century) lists by increasing difficulty a group of 21 authors: Donatus Grammarian, the *Disticha Catonis*, Aesopus, Avianus, Sedulius, Juvencus, Prosper of Aquitaine, Theodulus, Arator, Prudencius, Cicero, Sallust, Boethius, Lucanus, Ovidius, Juvenalis, Homer (in Latin translation), Persius, Statius, and as a colophon the classical author *par excellence* Vergilius." As an example, we copy below distichs 2-5: "2. Plus vigila semper nec somno deditus esto; / Nam diuturna quies vitiis alimenta ministrat. / 3. Virtutem primam esse puto compescere linguam: / Proximus ille deo est, qui scit ratione tacere. / 4. Sperne repugnando tibi tu contrarius esse: / Conveniet nulli, qui secum dissidet ipse. / 5. Si vitam inspicias hominum, si denique mores: / Cum culpant alios, nemo sine crimine vivit", which in Marchand's translation reads as follows: "2. Always keep alert, nor be given to sleep; / For continuous idleness offers food for vice. / 3. I think the first virtue to be keeping your tongue; / He is close to God who knows how to keep quiet properly. / 4. Avoid being strongly contrary to yourself; / He agrees with no one who disagrees with himself. / 5. If you look at the life of those (and their ways of life) / Who find fault with others, (you will find that) nobody is without fault".

As a second example of medieval aphoristic literature, also used in the school curriculum, we should mention another work with extremely wide dissemination throughout the Middle Ages and the Renaissance, the *Dicta et facta memorabilia* by Valerius Maximus (fl. 14-37 AD). This book was frequently utilized in an epitomized format by students for the exemplary value of the stories it contained, and as an anthology of moral behaviors useful for the Christian reader. Montaigne is said to have been very fond of Valerius's book. While many of the anecdotes in the book take the form of a long narrative, quite frequently with a very flourished style, short and epigrammatic aphorisms also abound.

During the Middle Ages, sapiential or wisdom literature was very much favoured in royal courts. It is usually defined as consisting of the discussions, sentences and statements by sages and philosophers about virtue and ethical, political, and religious matters usually within a narrative framework and the use of the techniques of traditional storytelling. The genre developed in the ancient Near East and it entered the western world through Islamic culture, where it also mixed with Greco-Roman traditions and evolved into subgenres such as the mirrors of princes. Within this genre we can place biblical wisdom literature encompassing the so-called five Sapiential Books, that is *The Book of Job, Proverbs, Ecclesiastes, Wisdom of Solomon, and Ecclesiasticus (Wisdom of Sirach)*, to which tradition has associated *Psalms* and *Song of Songs (Song of Solomon)*. In the Iberian Peninsula, for instance, gnomic literature was particularly abundant in the 13th and 14th centuries, with titles such as *Libro de los doce sabios, Poridat de poridades, Calila e Dimna, Doctrina d'en Pacs, Llibre de doctrina, Llibre de paraules i dits de savis i filòsofs, Secreto de los secretos, Paraules del rei Salomó, Libro de los buenos proverbios, Bocados de oro, Libro de los consejos, Llibre dels bons amonestaments, Flores de filosofía, Libro de los cien capítulos, Libro del consejo e de los consejeros*, and *Dichos de los santos padres*, among many other titles in Catalan, Castilian, and Portuguese literatures. Through these works, advice, maxims, aphorisms, adages, proverbs, and gnomic knowledge were transmitted on topics such as ethical behavior and social, governmental, and personal responsibility at large (Haro Cortés, Gómez Redondo).

Proverbs, Adages, and Emblems

With the advent of the Renaissance, maxims, proverbs, and aphorisms gained much acceptance in learned circles, to some extent as a continuation of the tradition of medieval sapiential literature and the rediscovery of classical philosophical works during the Humanism of the late Middle Ages. As an example, we can mention Hernán Núñez de Toledo's *Refranes o proverbios en romance* in the vernacular and Erasmus of Rotterdam's *Adagia* in Latin.

The humanist and classicist Hernán Núnez de Toledo (1475–1553), preceptor of Latin letters for the Tendilla household in Granada and later professor of rhetoric and Greek in Alcalá, is well known for his commentaries on the Juan de Mena's *Laberinto de Fortuna* and on Plinius the Elder (Weiss & Cortijo). In 1555, he published in Salamanca his *Refranes o proverbios en romance*, a collection of over 8,500 Spanish proverbs which included in most cases their equivalents in Catalan, Galician, Portuguese, French, Italian, Asturian, Latin, and Greek. This was the first work (together with Íñigo López de Mendoza's *Refranes que dizen las viejas tras el fuego*) of its kind in a vernacular Iberian language and exerted a great influence in later compilers of proverbs such as Juan de Mal Lara, César Oudin, Lorenzo Palmireno, etc. (Pla).

Refranes o proverbios en romance, Hernán Núñez, Lérida; A costa de Luys Manescal, 1621

This work reflected the new humanist trend of interest in *proverbia* (proverbs), usually defined as simple and insightful sayings of a purportedly traditional nature that express a perceived truth based on common sense or experience. On many occasions, proverbs use metaphorical and formulaic language. They were by no means new to the humanist period. For instance, the *Proverbia Grecorum* were compiled in the British Isles as early as the seventh or eighth centuries probably as a complement to the biblical *Book of Proverbs*. Collectanea of proverbs were also frequently used in the classroom throughout the Middle Ages. But it was Desiderius Erasmus of Rotterdam's (1466-1536) *Adagia* (*Collectanea Adagiorum*, Paris, 1500), a compilation of Greek and Latin proverbs later expanded to contain over three thousand, which became the work that inaugurated a trend of collecting and editing proverbs in many languages in books that often included essayistic commentaries on moral topics. Some examples of proverbs from the 1621 Robertson edition include "Sum egomet mihi Proximus, tunica pallio propior" (Close sitteth my shirt, but closer my skinne); "Prestat sero quan nunquam sapere" (Better late than neuer); "Cuique suum commentum placet" (Euery man after his fashion); "Ego de aliis loquor tu respondes de cepis" (I speake of wheate, and you of horse-corne); "Me mortuo terra misceatur incendio" (When I dye, the world dyeth with me), "Non luctu sed remedio opus in malis" (Sorrow neuer helped man); "Tempore prelustri fulmen ab arce venit" (Looke not to hye, lest a chip fall in your eye).

Next to adages, emblem books became one of the favourite genres of Renaissance and Baroque literature. An emblem book is a collection of emblems (allegorical illustrations) and mottos (short sentences or phrases that express a guiding moral maxim) together with a text that explains the connection between language and image. This explanation can range from a few lines to several pages of text either in verse or in prose. The first book of this kind was *Emblemata* (Augsburg, 1531) by Italian jurist Andrea Alciato (1492-1550), followed by countless others. The author referred to his book as a "learned recreation, a pastime for humanists steeped in classical culture". The connection with aphorisms in general can be seen in an example of this type of literature entitled *Moral emblems with aphorisms, adages, and proverbs, of all ages and nations*, by Jacob Cats and Robert Farlie (London, 1860). As an example of emblems, we will include the one entitled "Amicitia etiam post mortem durans" (Friendship lasts even after death), which is accompanied by a brief Latin poem: "Arentem senio, nudam quoque frondibus ulmum, / Complexa est viridi vitis opaca coma. / Agnoscitque vices naturae, & grata parenti, / Officii reddit mutua iura suo. / Exemploque monet, tales nos quaerere amicos, / Quos neque disiungat foedere summa dies" (A vine shady with green foliage embraced an elm tree that was dried up with age and bare of leaves. The vine recognizes the changes wrought by nature and, ever grateful, renders to the one that reared it the duty it owes in return. By the example it offers, the vine tells us to seek friends of such a sort that not even our final day will uncouple them from the bond of friendship).

Montaigne and the *Essai*

The French philosopher Michel Eyquem, Sieur de Montaigne (Michel de Montaigne) (1533–1592) is known for having popularized the essay as a literary genre. His *Essais* (first published in 1580) are composed of 107 chapters that vary in length. In the Preface to the Reader, Montaigne defines his writings in a manner closely resembling Joan Fuster's perception of his own work:

> I have proposed to myself no other than a domestic and private end: I have had no consideration at all either to thy service or to my glory. My powers are not capable of any such design. I have dedicated it to the particular commodity of my kinsfolk and friends, so that, having lost me (which they must do shortly), they may therein recover some traits of my conditions and humours, and by that means preserve more whole, and more life-like, the knowledge they had of me. Had my intention been to seek the world's favour, I should surely have adorned myself with borrowed beauties: I desire therein to be viewed as I appear in mine own genuine, simple, and ordinary manner, without study and artifice: for it is myself I paint. My defects are therein to be read to the life, and any imperfections and my natural form, so far as public reverence hath permitted me. If I had lived among those nations, which (they say) yet dwell under the sweet liberty of nature's primitive laws, I assure thee I would most willingly have painted myself quite fully and quite naked. Thus, reader, myself am the matter of my book: there's no reason thou shouldst employ thy leisure about so frivolous and vain a subject. (Cotton & Hazlitt)

In a frank and honest manner, with a rather didactic tone, Montaigne reflected in his essays on the nature of man and society, the physical world and the divine, offering a balanced or skeptical view on things. Critics have pointed out that Montaigne's method moved away from trying to prove an argument by *auctoritate* and instead attempted to explore its logical conclusions, frequently through an introspective language and tone that seem to suggest that he is dealing with the topics at hand in an inconsequential, unsure, and uncertain manner. He includes throughout his writings numerous quotes and maxims from Greek, Latin, and Italian authors. He also claims to have been very keen on numerous authors of *dicta et facta* and aphorisms, such as Seneca or Valerius Maximus, among many other classical philosophers. Two examples will suffice to illustrate Montaigne's style. In chapter V, when discussing "whether the governor of a place besieged ought himself to go out to parley", after reviewing the differences among Greek, Punic, and Roman customs on this matter, he indicates: "Deceit may serve for a need, but he only confesses himself overcome who knows he is neither subdued by policy nor misadventure, but by dint of valour, man to man, in a fair and just war". In chapter XXIV, speaking about pedantry, he quotes Du Bellay and Plutarch and engages in a dialogue with them by saying:

> I was often, when a boy, wonderfully concerned to see, in the Italian farces, a pedant always brought in for the fool of the play, and that the title of Magister was in no greater reverence amongst us: for being delivered up to their tuition, what could I do less than be jealous of their honour and reputation? I sought indeed to excuse them by the natural incompatibility betwixt the vulgar sort and men of a finer thread, both in judgment and knowledge, forasmuch as they go a quite contrary way to one another: but in this, the thing I most stumbled at was, that the finest gentlemen were those who most despised them; witness our famous poet Du Bellay—
>
> "Mais je hay par sur tout un savoir pedantesque" ["Of all things I hate pedantic learning."—Du Bellay]
>
> And 'twas so in former times; for Plutarch says that Greek and Scholar were terms of reproach and contempt amongst the Romans. But since, with the better experience of age, I find they had very great reason so to do, and that—
>
> "Magis magnos clericos non sunt magis magnos sapientes" ["The greatest clerks are not the wisest men," a proverb given in Rabelais' *Gargantua*, i. 39.]
>
> But whence it should come to pass, that a mind enriched with the knowledge of so many things should not become more quick and sprightly, and that a gross and vulgar understanding should lodge within it, without correcting and improving itself, all the discourses and judgments of the greatest minds the world ever had, I am yet to seek.
> **This last paragraph is also a quote from Montaigne**

Friedrich Nietzsche

Last but not least in this succinct overview of aphoristic literature, the German philosopher Friedrich Nietzsche (1844–1900) claimed to utilize aphorisms because while seemingly simple they allowed for irony, sarcasm, and nuanced interpretations, thus offering the possibility to explore deeper meanings. A classical philologist, he is known to have had deep admiration for Heraclitus (to whom he devoted his doctoral dissertation) and Montaigne, from whom he probably acquired a taste for pithy aphorisms and an essayistic style of writing in short paragraphs. His work is generally considered a critique of religion, morality, and the foundations of Christianity, aptly summarized by the paradoxical and disorienting statement "God is dead". As some critics have concluded, while some of Nietzsche's books have a greater continuity of thought (particularly *The Birth of Tragedy*, *On the Genealogy of Morality*, and *The Antichrist*), "even there, he will often take advantage of section breaks to drop one thread of reasoning and move on to apparently unrelated points, leaving the reader to piece together how the various aspects of his case are supposed to fit together … *Thus Spoke Zarathustra* is unified by following the career of a central character, but the unity is loose and picaresque-like—a sequence of episodes which arrives at a somewhat equivocal (or at a minimum, at a controversial) conclusion that imposes only weak narrative unity on the whole. This mode of writing is often classified as 'aphoristic'" (Anderson). Some of his aphorisms include: "When you gaze long into an abyss the abyss also gazes into you"; "Become who you are"; "It is not a lack of love, but a lack of friendship that makes unhappy marriages"; "Become who you are"; "My formula for greatness in a human being is *amor fati*: that one wants nothing to be different, not forward, not backward, not in all eternity"; "Ultimately, it is the desire, not the desired, that we love"; "There is always some madness in love. But there is also always some reason in madness"; "Whoever does not have two-thirds of his day for himself, is a slave, whatever he may be: a statesman, a businessman, an official, or a scholar"; "We often contradict an opinion for no other reason than that we do not like the tone in which it is expressed"; "I mistrust all systematizers and avoid them. The will to a system is a lack of integrity."

Ramón Gómez de la Serna

Spanish avant-garde writer Ramón Gómez de la Serna (1888–1963) was the creator of a genre often referred to as *greguerías*, which has been translated into English as "one-liners" or more accurately as "aphorisms". Greguerías **last word should be in italics** were defined by the author himself as "humor plus metaphor". These are poetic, humorous, and often seemingly incongruent sentences (sometimes longer) that express a philosophical idea in a witty and original manner. Some examples include "The peacock is a retired myth" (El pavo real es un mito jubilado); "Doors get angry with the wind" (Las puertas se enfadan con el viento); "Fragrance is the flowers' echo" (El perfume es el eco de las flores).

Finally, Fuster

Joan Fuster followed as avowed referents in his use of aphorisms several of the authors we have analyzed above, notably Heraclitus, Montaigne, Nietzsche, or Gómez de la Serna. Emphasizing the essay as his favorite genre, his conception of literature can be summarized with the words *engaging* and *skepticism*. In Vicent Salvador's words, it "combines the intrinsic values of literature as an autonomous domain and ethical engagement with historical social change… Fuster makes no systematic analysis of literature in any of the numerous pages he wrote because he is not an academic theoretician" (22). Fuster's main intention was to raise awareness as a sort of ethical prophet, and, as Salvador goes on to say:

> On these occasions, Fuster seems to succumb to the temptation of expressive brilliance and prefers an immediate dramatic impact to the precision of conceptual nuances. After all, this is the price that the essayist has to pay for a flowing discourse, which is contaminated by the journalistic style and the sententiousness of aphorism. (124)

We can conclude by saying that Fuster's use of aphorisms, in addition to the intrinsic value they provide to his conception of literature, is part of a long tradition that goes back to classical times and has been present in Western philosophical and essayistic writings ever since. Fuster is simply one of the most illustrious representatives of their use.

Vicent Salvador

(Universidad Jaume I, †)

Fuster and Aphorisms

The books *Consells, proverbis i insolències* (*Advice, Proverbs, and Insolences*), together with *Nosaltres, els valencians* (*We, the Valencians*), and *Diccionari per a ociosos* (*Dictionary for the Idle*) are among the most representative examples of Fuster's production (1922/1992). *Nosotros, los valencianos* is a radiography of Valencian society from the point of view of its history and sociological identity, a book that was fundamental for subsequent theorizations on the Pays Valencià (Valencian Nation) within the context of the Països Catalans (Catalan-speaking Nation(s)). His *Dictionary for the Idle*, inspired by Voltaire's *Dictionnaire philosophique portatif* (Portable Philosophical Dictionary), gathers a collection of short essays professing to be pleasant and intellectually stimulating for a plurality of readers, and has been Fuster's most translated work: into Spanish [*Diccionario para ociosos*, Península, 1970], English [*Dictionary for the Idle*, Sheffield Academic Press,1992], Italian [*Dizionario per oziosi*, Tullio Pironti ed., 1994], and French [*Dictionnaire à l'usage des oisifs*, Anacharsis, 2010].

The book *Consejos, proverbios e insolencias* is not a book dealing with the identity of a nation nor is it as "exportable" as the *Dictionary for the Idle*, for which reason it has not been fortunate enough to have been translated into other European languages. Nevertheless, it is the epitome of Fuster's aphoristic writing, a brilliant exercise of syncopated and deep thought that aspires to have a degree of universality. On one hand, it is part of an old tradition of sapiential literature as well as of more modern traditions, such as those of French *moralists* like Chamfort, La Rochefoucauld, Joubert, or other European writers like Nietzsche, Paul Valéry, or Cioran… (Mautner 1985). This list could also include Catalan names like Santiago Rusiñol or Eugeni D'Ors. But as we will see, Fuster's aphorisms have a very characteristic personal profile.

As he himself confessed, his penchant for writing aphorisms accompanied him for a long time as a peculiar *hobby*. In fact, before publishing *Judicis finals* (*Final Judgements*), he had published several aphorisms in Latin American journals of the Catalan exile (*La Nostra Revista*, *Pont Blau*). He also published some in Catalan journals like *L'Espill*, which he directed at the time: in fact, a group of them later became part of one of his last essays, *Sagitari*. Even posthumously,

Francesc Pérez Moragón and Josep Palacios released a previously unknown group of great interest: *Bestiari*.

Consejos, proverbios e insolencias (*Advice, Proverbs and Insolences*) was published in 1968 by AC and is composed of two parts: "Final Judgements", published previously in Majorca by Moll (1960), and "Indecent Proposals", which was unpublished until that moment. As can be noticed, the titles of the book and its parts are highly indicative: "Judicis finals" plays on the ambiguity of the first word, which can be understood as "opinions" as well as being influenced by the Biblical phrase "final judgement", now in plural. In the second part, "proposicions" can be interpreted as the plural of proposition (the content of a statement), as well as "proposal", "request", and thus by adding the idea of dishonesty it can refer to proposals of an erotic nature, traditionally considered illicit and transgressive.

The title of the volume, on the other hand, puts together semantically three types of verbal activities: advising, stating expressions coined as popular wisdom, and daring, nerve, or even insult. Giving advice is a verbal action that involves risk if the person offering it is not morally competent to do so nor has he been asked. Accordingly, it involves a risk of a social nature for him who dares to give advice on his own. Proverbs refer to anonymous, collective, and pluri-secular elaboration (the wisdom of tradition), which does not apply to this case; insolences are clearly a transgression of what is proper and of political correctness. The combination of semantic references in the title suggests the idea of a transgressing provocation.

Deep down, the main paradox is derived from the fact that Fuster's aphorisms are not anonymous statements—which are generally endowed with a conservative character—like refrains but rather the work of a contemporary author playing with irony and offering content that is somewhat subversive. Nonetheless, we should bear in mind that Fuster uses the rhetorical device of the voice of traditional wisdom, which gives him added *auctoritas*.

The humanism that characterizes Fuster's production, especially his essays, is rationalistic, critical, and mostly heterodox. Its textual style combines a wise combination of three elements: laconic succinctness, irony, and a tinge of conversationalism (Salvador 1994, 2008). His humanism must be placed within a philosophical tradition that includes authors such as Montaigne, Voltaire, Bertrand Russell—whom he qualifies as a "disinfectant" of all metaphysics—or even the philosophical humanism of William James.

Thus, his aphorisms do not contradict that intellectual attitude, although, needless to say, they must be expressed in a truncated manner with no room for explicative descriptions or nuances that serve to make ideas more precise.

Fuster's essays are full of sententious sentences that, when isolated from their context, could be read as aphorisms, although the flow of discourse allows him enough space to justify his assertions, make his sentences more precise, or even contradict them—things that are more difficult in succinct aphoristic writing. The challenge with aphorisms is precisely to cultivate a dialectical laconism that can be provocative without falling into the dogmatic tone of the writer who pontificates about life and the world.

Aphoristic literature consciously accepts being subjected to the laws of a strict *brevitas* that limits the reduction of discourse to small snippets of thought which are easier to memorize but more difficult to uncritically accept because of the forcefulness, not duly justified, of their value judgements.

The brevity of these microtexts, on the other hand, must be compensated for with intense and thorough construction: the labor of a goldsmith of language, similar to that of a lyric poet. Words in aphorisms, due to their subjection to *brevitas*, must serve a concentrated and distilled discourse, like an intense and highly valuable perfume; in addition, they must be articulated with clockwork precision. In a certain way, aphoristic texts are a sort of experiment in a verbal laboratory where words are observed through a microscope, analyzed with precise instruments, treated with properly dosed chemical reactants and following certain protocols before being handled.

If we deprive them of that expressive tension that surprises readers with unusual images and an ending that forces them to reflect, an aphorism would just be a catechetical maxim, or a banal exercise of unsubstantial and cliché statements, such as a badly delivered joke that makes listeners shrug their shoulders or think "so what?".

Aphorisms contain a *sententia* in the sense of a result of a previous debate, as it occurs in legal milieus. In this case, it is the author who has debated a topic with himself or with the proposals of the authors he mentions, and his critical reflection leads him to a well-meditated conclusion. In addition, this conclusion does not want to be simply imposed upon but leaves the door open to being assimilated and discussed by the reader. For Fuster, the main pedagogical concern of a writer of aphorisms is to make the reader reflect, thus transforming the slogan of doctrinary maxims into the proposal of a conundrum that readers must resolve by themselves, accepting or rejecting its ultimate meaning. Without a doubt, it is something similar to a riddle or a puzzle where the result is not necessarily the only possible solution. Sometimes even the writer himself proposes alternative conclusions either within the aphorism or in subsequent texts that seem to dialogue with each other. He does so frequently through counter-argumentative connectors ("but", "nevertheless"), concesivity ("despite", "in any case", "be that as it may"...) or expressions that have a deeper meaning different from the obvious one: "fundamentally", "deep down", "ultimately"....

The prologue to the book generously offers suggestions on many of these issues, like snippets of a real aphorism theory. We can focus, for instance, on a biographical anecdote about young Fuster: his fascination with the Almanac of the Sacred Heart of Jesus, where its Jesuit author proposed a new thought to consider on every page for the corresponding day. The anecdote sheds light on Fuster's particular conception of his own reception theory. Certainly, the aphoristic discourse here does not lend itself to a fast reading, which would result in a heap of ideas lumped together that are difficult to digest, but rather elicits the opposite: an unhurried reception determined by the arrival of a new day with a meditated and very personal reception.

The slow rhythm of reception fosters, on one hand, a possible memorization of the microtext, which can be repeated at successive moments and therefore internalized. At the same time, and because of it, the slow rhythm promotes a critical assimilation of its content. Of course, we are not dealing with slogans intended for blind obedience like those of a televangelist, but rather some sort of enigma, a subjective and problematic statement that the reader will have to solve and freely accept or reject, imagining other alternatives. The reader that Fuster has in mind is to be surprised, almost stunned, by an unexpected proposal, a daring metaphor similar to an incredible horse jump, and his foreseeable reaction is to realign himself and apply his own sight to the proposal in order to reposition himself within the world of ideas.

Perhaps it is useful to remember that the large typological variety of aphorisms that have abounded in our culture can be associated with two distinct strategic categories: the most traditional one, endowed with deep seriousness and mostly associated with conservative thought; and the other pole, pure wit that activates a verbal juggling close to poetic and humorous play. It fluctuates between the moral maxim and the linguistic play of an imaginative character that refuses to transmit any doctrine whatsoever. The most obvious factor shared by both strategies is what we can term the "memorable density" of those microtexts. A characteristic example of the second type is the *greguería*, a genre cultivated by the Spanish writer Ramón Gómez de la Serna. Of course, there are many instances of a combination of both strategies, as is the case with authors such as Musil, Canetti, Bergamín, Antonio Machado or Nietzsche himself.

We also find in Fuster's works examples of the option of mere verbal play that usually utilizes metaphors, metonymies, and synaesthesias. One case illuminates this idea: "Rameau's harpsichord has a toothache". Nevertheless, Fuster usually prefers to give precedence to conceptual content and reflections that seek depth, as he confesses in the prologue to this book when he states that he has tried to avoid the imprudence of making aphorisms be a pure witty exercise at the expense of what we could term the pedagogical seriousness and utility of his intentional program of making readers conscious through his personal mayeutics.

That said, that compromise with the social usefulness of aphorisms does not bring Fuster closer to the bombastic depth associated with ideological immobilism. It is not about assuming the shared *doxa* in order to persuade in the most efficacious manner but rather the opposite: it is about subverting it by positioning oneself very close to heterodoxy. By dismantling linguistic clichés and thinking routines, Fuster makes aphorisms build unsettling paradoxes. Thus, for instance, he wonders whether the proverbial fidelity of dogs towards their owners could not be interpreted as a case of self-interested adulation. Or he can turn an idiom upside down—and the corresponding automatism of a way of thinking imposed by social convention—in the case of "whoever pays is in charge" and capture, with a play on words, a new idea that has the obvious intention of social critique: "Is whoever pays really in charge? History and daily experience show, at least, that those in command are reimbursed. To command is to be reimbursed—among other things."

To some extent, this mechanism is similar to the defamiliarization and automatization that were so aptly and extensively used by Russian formalism. Certainly, the aphoristic genre can claim for itself the category of literary genre and in some aspects it comes close to poetic expression. Precisely for this reason, the author has considered aphorisms as a sort of "frustrated epigrams". But in this case the main point is the idea, beyond the verbal play or aesthetic emotion: Fuster's work, like his essays, is *literature of ideas*, conceptual gymnastics, a machine to produce knowledge that aims to shake conventional inertias in order to awaken sleeping consciousness. In this sense, Fuster's pen wants to *deconstruct* traditional aphorisms through a clearly subversive manipulation, in a sense like the Éluard's and Péret's surrealism in their *152 proverbes mis au goût du jour* (Grésillon & Maingueneau 1984).

Throughout his deconstructive work, Fuster focuses on lexical language structures, such as when he says that "people are them", with a tacit exclusion of those who use the ambiguous term "people". Or he denounces lexical ageing as when he affirms that *nowadays* adultery (note: he is writing this in the 1950s) seems like a corny expression. He acts as a lexical hygienist and astute observer of the ideological adherences that words have undergone throughout the social history of the language is, undoubtedly, very remarkable, to the point that a scholar like Amadeu Viana (1987) has even affirmed that Fuster's aphorisms are, in essence, a study of discourse, although one written in "colloquial language".

Certainly, conversationalism, which is one of the most characteristic elements of Fuster's style in his essays, is not absent from his aphorisms. On the contrary, both the syncopated syntax of these texts and the interjections and exclamations, or even the colloquial register of many words, are evidence of a desire to express himself in a familiar manner, as if he were in a conversation with himself or the reader. The discourse abounds in questions, doubts, self-corrections, and appeals to the reader to whom he advises, or to his alter ego, who refutes or questions his own assertions, as if it were a dialogue in front of a mirror. This conversational tone is the best antidote against solemn dogmatism or excessive sententiousness, the major temptations in this genre.

Nonetheless, emphasizing this colloquial tone as the sole element of a dialogical intent does not do justice to the powerful rhetorical machinery that Fuster puts in motion in his aphorisms with the intention of *delectare et prodesse* (or of *prodesse* through the practice of *delectare*).

One of these rhetorical mechanisms is the intense intertextuality demonstrated by Fuster's aphorisms, especially in the first part of the book, "Final Judgements". Indeed, the text frequently refers back to previous texts that the author quotes, glosses, or contradicts. It is a type of dialogism that critics have not always been able to analyze properly, where Fuster engages with other authors from the cultural tradition and from numerous genres. Renan, for instance, seems like a nun to him; Proust's work is a repetitive reading in many regards, like chewing gum repeatedly. Valéry seems a cold poet to him: "diamonds are not edible"... In these instances, the author is not excessively respectful and displays a critical temperament with a touch of insolence.

On other occasions, his attitude is not critical; rather, he simply takes some author's quote or reference as a starting point to develop his own proposal: "Just as poor King Lear asked: 'Who is it that can tell who I am?'" Or he makes a reference to Descartes and creates a *contrafactum* of his famous sentence: "If you are paid, you do exist".

In any case, many aphorisms resemble marginal notes, as pointed out excellently by Carme Gregori-Soldevila when highlighting their character as "marginalia" that refers back to other historical periods of the genre, such as when, during the 16th and 17th centuries, aphorisms appeared on the margins of other people's works, especially in translations of Tacitus: a sort of glosses or commentaries like those that according to Spanish historians appear early on in writings from the monasteries of Silos or San Millán de la Cogolla.

On the other hand, the marginality or subaltern condition of aphorisms is reflected in the peripheral condition frequently attributed to them in literature as "minor" writing, not very relevant in the republic of letters. Within Fuster's production, this genre is, for some critics, something secondary, lower-case writing so to speak within his paramount essays. Nevertheless, the significance of this chapter of his legacy cannot be denied, and it complements other genres and fields of thought, such as his work as a committed historian or his reflections as a theoretician of nationalism. If for Fuster writing essays allows him to feel free like one who practices "shirtsleeves" writing, constructing these precious creatures must have made him feel even freer, like one who writes in his "undershirt" at home. Notwithstanding, his destiny and vocation are ultimately to be an author of public writing.

Besides this frequent intertextual play, the powerful rhetorical machinery of Fuster's aphorisms functions with many other strategies. For instance, metaphors transform the reader's perception of reality, such as defending that marriage is the only legal form of complicity accepted by society, or that love is just one more among venereal diseases, or that "all ideas end up suffering from rheumatism". Very frequently metaphors and comparisons, like in the aforementioned instances, start from a "biologistic" vision of abstractions. Certainly, one of Fuster's recurrent ideas is a conscious materialistic perspective on life, not only *historical* materialism but one with a biological approach, which makes us see ideas and behaviours through a somatic lens.

Many of these surprising analogies appear either explicitly or as hypotheses and suggestions through resources endowed with a conversational tone: "To a certain degree, all paintings are a self-portrait"; "And are we not all apocryphal characters?"; "And chastity, what about it? Is it not a form of avarice?"

Another rhetorical weapon is irony, which sometimes verges on cynicism: "Amphitruo invites you for dinner. Say: Long live Amphitruo!"; "Do not be insolent. They will think you are sincere!" In addition, classical rhetorical figures abound in the book: paronomasias, praeteritions, antitheses, or puns, such as: "Books do not *substitute* life, but life does not substitute books either". Fuster's aphorisms would be excellent examples for students of the tropes and figures explained in handbooks of rhetoric.

A special place is occupied by paradoxes (which reflect the complexity of the meaning of life and of making assertions), which permits seeing life from seemingly contradictory perspectives: "The most difficult body part to convince is the genitalia. Or the easiest—it depends on how you look at it". Sometimes the seeming contradiction is not made explicit, as in the last example, but the truth is that Fuster repeatedly dwells on paradoxes, perspectives that are both possible although hardly compatible. Readers have the last word in these cases and must provide answers to questions that shake everyone's intellectual security.

Regarding what we could term the narrative framework of aphoristic texts, it can adopt different forms: besides the definitions provided earlier, it can consist of general assertions, direct appeals to the reader (advice, chastisement, etc.), exclamations that express wishes or fears, or confessions of an *I* presented as a prototype of the human condition: "I am perpetually convalescing from my prejudices".

On the other hand, many aphoristic texts begin with a connector (for instance, "and besides", "in any case"…) that sometimes seems to refer to a previous aphorism and other times to an indefinite and imprecise context: "And you? Are you not bad company?". In the latter cases, the reader perceives that the aphorism is part of a tacit or implicit conversation between him and the author. It would be too lengthy to indicate exhaustively all the nuances of the narrative frameworks present in Fuster's voice as a writer of aphorisms.

In any case, as pointed out by Ruth Amossy (2006), the unexpected figure—as opposed to the *cliché* that helps convince the ingenuous—creates a more or less violent rupture from previous expectations, reorganizing the order of the discourse. What is relevant is that this strategy is geared towards making the reader feel and think for himself.

Under the apparent simplicity of the aphoristic play, the truth is that the brief texts of the book—just like the rest of Fuster's aphoristic production—form a sort of play in which the characters are heterogeneous voices, masks, quotes, and evocations. Under the guise of a sapiential tone used as an excuse and a persuasive weapon, the author-playwright composes a polyphonic piece, constructing a machine that shreds discourses, contrasts, caricatures, or discredits them with a planned subversion of the inertias of thought and language.

Works Cited

Alciato at Glasgow. https://www.emblems.arts.gla.ac.uk/alciato/.

Alvar Nuño, Guillermo, & Elena Borsari eds. *The Classsics During the Middle Ages*. Leiden: Brill, In press.

Amossy, R. *L'argumentation dans le discours*. Paris: Armand Colin, 2006.

Anderson, R. Lanier. "Friedrich Nietzsche". In *The Stanford Encyclopedia of Philosophy* (Summer 2022 Edition). Edward N. Zalta ed. https://plato.stanford.edu/archives/sum2022/entries/nietzsche/.

Barnes, J. *The Presocratic Philosophers*. London: Routledge & Kegan Paul, 1982.

Erasmus, Desiderius. *Adages*. In *Collected Works of Erasmus*. Trans. R.A.B Mynors et al. Toronto: University of Toronto Press, 1982–2006. Vols. 31–36.

———. *Adagia in Latine and English containing five hundred proverbs: very profitable for the vse of those who aspire to further perfection in the Latine tongue*. Bartholomew Robertson ed. London: Printed by Bernard Alsop, dwelling in Distaff-Lane, at the signe of the Dolphine, 1621

———. *Moral emblems with aphorisms, adages, and proverbs, of all ages and nations*, by Jacob Cats and Robert Farlie. London: Longman, Green, Longman, and Roberts, 1860.

Etymological Dictionary of Greek. Robert Neekes ed. Leiden: Brill, 2010. 2 vols.

Gómez Redondo, Fernando. *Historia de la prosa medieval castellana.1. La creación del discurso prosístico: el entramado cortesano*. Madrid: Cátedra, 1998.

———. *Vol. II: El desarrollo de los géneros. La ficción caballeresca y el orden religioso*. Madrid: Cátedra, 1999.

———. *Vol. III: Los orígenes del humanismo. El marco cultural de Enrique III y Juan II*. Madrid: Cátedra, 2002.

Gómez de la Serna, Ramón. *Aphorisms*. Miguel Gonzalez-Gerth tr. Pittsburgh: Latin American Literary Review Press, 1989.

Graham, Daniel W. "Heraclitus". In *The Stanford Encyclopedia of Philosophy* (Summer 2021 Edition), Edward N. Zalta ed. https://plato.stanford.edu/archives/sum2021/entries/heraclitus/.

———. "Heraclitus and Parmenides." In *Presocratic Philosophy: Essays in Honour of Alexander Mourelatos*. V. Caston and D. W. Graham eds. Aldershot: Ashgate, 2002. 27–44.

Gregori-Soldevila, C. *Anotacions al marge. Els aforismes de Joan Fuster*. València: Publicacions de la Universitat de València, 2011.

Grésillon, Alain & Dominique Maingueneau. "Polyphonie, proverbe et détournement; ou un proverbe peut cacher un autre." *Langages* 73 (1984): 25–53.

Haro Cortés, Marta. "El viaje sapiencial en la prosa didáctica castellana de la Edad Media". *Actas del Primer congreso Anglo-Hispano*. Madrid: Castalia, 1993. II, 59–72.

Hippocrates *Collected Works I*. Hippocrates. W. H. S. Jones ed. Cambridge: Harvard University Press, 1868.

———. *Corpvs medicorvm Graecorvm / Latinorvm*. https://cmg.bbaw.de/epubl/online/editionencmg_01.html

Kirk, G. S. *Heraclitus: The Cosmic Fragments*. Cambridge: Cambridge University Press.

Lacarra, María Jesús, and Francisco López Estrada. *Orígenes de la prosa*. Madrid: Júcar, 1993.

Lacarra, María Jesús. *Cuento y novela corta en España, 1. Edad Media.* Barcelona: Crítica, 1999.

Mautner, Franz H. "Der Aphorismus". In Klaus Weissenberger ed. *Prosakunst ohne Erzählen*, Tübingen: Niemeyer, 1985. 7–26.

Montaigne, Michel de. *Essays.* Translated by Charles Cotton. Edited by William Carew Hazlitt. London: Reeves and Turner, 1877. https://www.gutenberg.org/files/3600/3600-h/3600-h.htm

Núñez de Toledo, Hernán (Comendador Griego). *Refranes o proverbios en romance (1555) de Hernán Núñez.* Edición crítica de Louis Combet, Julia Sevilla, Germán Conde y Josep Guia. Madrid: Ediciones Guillermo Blázquez, 2001. 2 vols.

——. *Refranes o proverbios en romance.* Lérida; A costa de Luys Manescal, 1621.

Oxford English Dictionary. https://www.oed.com/.

Philips, Margaret Mann. *The Adages of Erasmus.* Cambridge: Cambridge University Press, 1964,

Pla Codomer, Francisco Pedro. "'Refranes o proverbios en romance' de Hernán Núñez (II): traducción, equivalencia y fraseometría de los refranes gallegos y catalanes!. *Rhythmica* 19 (2021): 129–166.

Salvador, Vicent. "Fuster's Conception of Literature as a Social Practice". *Jorunal of Catalan Intellectual History* 11 (2017): 122–133.

——. "Els mots de Joan Fuster". In Manuel Pérez-Saldanya (ed.) *Joan Fuster: lengua i estil.* València: Publicacions de la Universitat de València, 2008. 13–31.

——. *Fuster o l'estratègia del centaure*, València: Bullent, 1994.

Tous Prieto, Francesc. "El proverbi en context: teoría i práctica de les formes sentencioses medievals". *Els Marges* 109 (2016): 10–30.

Viana, Amadeu. "Fuster *in fabula*". *Els Marges* 38 (1987): 33–43.

Weiss, Julian, & Antonio Cortijo Ocaña eds. *Glosa sobre las Trezientas.* Madrid: Polifemo, 2015.

APHORISMS

Final Judgments[1]

Prejudices

It is written: «Judge not lest ye be judged» (or perhaps: «Judge not and you shall not be judged»; I cannot remember). Well. Nevertheless, in whatever shape or form, it seems that we shall be—and we are already—necessarily judged. As for us, why then deprive us of the pleasure of judging others?

You already know the renowned Greek aphorism: «Joan Fuster is the measure of all things».

I defend a methodical distrust, nonetheless.

Knowing What I am Talking About

«I am not claiming to be right, what I say is that that's how I am», said Paul Valéry as if offering a excuse for himself. Perhaps it could have been simply said—in fact it can be said—: «I am right because that's how I am».

Everything we do is irreversible.

Our joys are usually based on ridiculously banal motives. This is rather sad if we analyze it coldly.

Always demand the right to change your opinion: that is the first that your enemies will deny you.

We also get tired from waiting.

We will not know a person until we see them out of control.

---

[1] "Final judgments" play on the ambiguity of the expression, which might refer to the biblical "final judgment" of God at the end of times, or it can be understood as the author's "final opinion" on many topics, or even as "the definite and final opinion" that could possibly be had on any topic (with an authoritarian tinge to it), or even as the "final sentence" (on an opinion) passed by a judge/censor of thoughts (the author himself).

Some affirm—I am sure they have their reasons to do so—that man is a contingent being. As for myself, I can only say that if I did not exist, it would be necessary to invent me.

It is useless to make a joke about it; we will never understand how it is to be Persian.

Item more: how can there be someone different than me?, how can someone be another-the other?

If common sense—what we call common sense—were really common, we would become crazy.

Euphemisms are in themselves a lie.

Shakespeare did not have to work very hard to be Shakespeare, nor Goethe to be Goethe or Dante to be Dante. And that is slightly discouraging.

Many love wounds are just wounds of our self-esteem.

When has a secret, a personal confession to a friend not been motivated by vanity? Even when great atrocities are being confessed.

We are always stupid compared to someone.

I ignore whether the obsession with death, which is so typical of teenagers, belongs to the chapter on depravity or that on conceit.

Word was given to men not to reveal or hide their thoughts, rather to justify them.

Becoming old is resigning yourself to becoming old. There is no other explanation for it.

In any event, it is recommended to grow old at the same rate as your body.

Audaces fortuna iuvat.[2]— Gods help those who are bold just out of humor.

To be friends with someone who is very selfish—more selfish than ourselves—makes things easier. It allows us to simulate friendship without remorse.

Gratitude cripples.

---

2 "Fortune helps those who are bold".

«Our desire knows no remedy», exclaimed somewhere St. Therese of Avila. That is in fact a great truth, at least literally. And taking it as a premise, all sillogisms that derive from it can only reach one conclusion: «Life is useless».

Love.— Despite everything, in Dante's style: *Io son più ch'io*[3]...

Thought affirms itself—and stands firm—through objections. Give me a good *opponent* and I will be able to come up with the most remarkable theories.

Just as poor King Lear asked: «Who is it that can tell who I am».

It seems nonsense, but the first requirement to be a cynic is that the others are not.

There is a «fear of knowledge», which is the fear of becoming—or converting into— what we are knowing.

«...Human, too human...».

There is nothing that is *too* human.

Nothing can be had—*grabbed*: freedom or power, happines or things, love—, unless taken from another.

«Discussion begets light», they say. And experience shows that indeed everyone seems to remain with the same convictions he had before the discussion began, although they are more clear now.

It is part of a good education to know when it is fitting to not be impolite.

We are unique.

Blessed are those who have had a teacher—meaning obviously *maître à penser*[4]—, because they will be able to deny him.

We must take things as they are—and consequently death, suffering and injustice—that is as the demiurges' blackmail.

Pretending to give up can be, when considered closely, an excellent resourse for a politician as well as for a lover.

Of our enemies, we do not envy their flaws, almost always and of course *sub specie boni*. It is their virtues that, deep down, we hate and what bothers us.

In my case, alcohol makes me more understanding.

---

3   *Paradiso* XVI, 18. "I am more than just myself".
4   A teacher whom one chooses, a mentor.

That character by Balzac who aspired to «live excessively», I cannot understand it, my Lord, for I would like, etc.

Perhaps we are never as sincere as when we pretend to be sincere.

«Elephants are contagious», said a surrealist. And perhaps he was right. You never know.

For something to be able to move us, it must contain a certain dose of vulgarity.

Man has done nothing else since he is man: to amend creation, to correct God's work—everything God had made and that, according to Genesis, he considered good…

When one reaches the conclusion that a problem has no solution, one becomes a slave. Hence a *fatality* is born that can be properly termed tragic, which, in fact, is the fatality of the old tragedies.

Give a mistake an axiomatic formulation and it will end up seeming a truth to you.

Only death is perfect, and even then not always.

All my ideas are provisional. (Let it be known that I am not proud about this).

If you think about it, you will realize that it really does not bother you to be contradicted but rather to be made aware that you are contradicting yourself.

The capacity to forget something is undoubtedly a clear sign of good physical and moral health..

The world would be much more intolerable if one—I, you, he—did not believe that their own life is exceptional.

Furtive loves have this good thing: they end up seeming charming to us.

«I do not despise almost anything (Je ne méprise presque rien)…». Neither do I—and you can forgive me.

If it seems that sometimes you agree with someone, do not doubt: there has been a misunderstanding.

Women are pure physiology: Men also, but they strive to hide it.

I imagine that there is some sort of difference between being an atheist with regard to Jehovah and being an atheist with regard to any other divinity (or regarding a sincere Olympus).

Besides, I think we should not confuse two things as different as atheism and xenophobia. More than one *soi disant* atheist is nothing but a more or less enraged theofobe.

All men are mortal, and I more than anyone.

Author's modesty— Aphorisms—mine and everybody else's—are always false, intrinsically false. So is this one.

It is dangerous to gain the enmity of someone stupid because stupid people are usually more harmful than the wicked ones. In addition, it is also more uncomfortable from a moral standpoint to have a stupid person as our enemy, we always feel that we look ridiculous.

We can only be refuted by one who thinks like us.

Any ambition, no matter how murky, can be respected if taken to a violent extreme.

—What—Time.

And indeed time *passes*.[5]

Every name is a pseudonym; every face is a mask; every gesture, an affectation; every word a misunderstanding. And in these conditions, man is a social animal! Yes, my dears, *zoon politikon*.

«Ego dixi: Dii estis»[6] (Ps., lxxxi, 6). And we do not want to believe it!

The most useful lessons are those we decide not to follow, precisely because we do not profit from them.

If an adult misses his childhood it is because he does not remember it or hardly remembers it.

We must denounce that under the innocence of the Abels there is, quite frequently, a blatantly outrageous provocation. Rather, that innocence *per se* is in most cases a provocation.

---

5   The original includes a play on words based on the verb *passar*. *Passar* denotes the passing of time, passing by somewhere, and in the expression *què passa*, it means "what's up".

6   "I said: ye are gods"

All metaphysics are «consolation metaphysics», including Camus's, inasmuch as it is metaphysical.

That is why I believe that there is not much difference, *from the consumer's point of view*, between philosophy and brandy or morphine.

Some people are lawyers, teachers, politicans, bishops, poets, farmers. My profession instead is being Joan Fuster.

For many things, but especially love, experience is usually a flaw. Thus why the first love is remembered as the best one—it is in fact the best one.

We only say—and write!—platitudes: otherwise we would not understand each other.

The truth in school.— «Adaequatio intellectus et rei». We agree: but what is the meaning of *adaequatio*?, and what is the meaning of *intellectus*?, and what is the meaning of *rei*? And even, what is the meaning of *et*?

There are no different ways of believing.

Nobody offends us more than he who refuses to be our enemy, particularly when we wish him to be our enemy.

Life is monotonous, no doubt, and to a large degree, but we do not usually realize that we are ourselves even more monotonous.

Topic for meditation.—*At this very moment*, there are millions and millions of people who are fornicating in thought, word, and deed; the other millions are waiting for their opportunity to do so. (That *moment* in question is always any moment.)

Other people's vanity is *only* unbearable to us because we consider it an usurpation.

Pay close attention: we always do God's will—the will of another.

«Duo si idem dicunt, non est idem[7]». But even more: the same thing, said by the same person in a different moment, is not the same anymore.

We know we must die, but the instinct of preservation recommends us to forget it.

---

7 "If two say the same, it is not the same".

A systematic thought, that is one that has no internal contradictions, will always have the disadvantage of being unable to solve its contradiction with life.

consells, proverbis i insolències

There is a danger: that of ending up being similar to yourself. Although it is also rather difficult to imitate yourself.

Le moi haïssable.[8]— I am not a prudent man: I have not stooped so low. I am just a coward, which is something entirely different—and to a certain extent the opposite.

From time to time, we feel the need to create a Manichean so that we can give ourselves the pleasure of refuting him. If we did not do this, we would end up loosing our faith in our own convictions.

The fact that man has been able to invent through the centuries so many metaphysical theories is something that should not surprise us. Deep down, they are just an excrescence of our imagination. What is somehow more surprising and even alarming is that man *has needed or still needs* to invent them.

Ah, if only the sex could think!

(My apologies, Pascal suggested it to me: «Imagine a body full of thinking members…».)

There is death: so there will always be God. There is life: so there will always be gods.

Rarely can a truth be stated—some types of truth anyway—without it seeming insolent.

Perhaps because of this, sometimes, there are those who seemingly tell the truth by their insolence.

The possessives: here you have some grammatical forms that are truly perturbing.

We give importance, much importance, to certain things *so that* we can believe that in this desolate life there are important things.

All theories, when taken to their last consequences, are absurd. That means that they *were so* from the beginning, at least in part. We cannot say that this

---

8 "My hateful self", a variation of the usual Franch saying, "The I is hateful".

conclusion should take us to practice a moderate skepticism. To practice it, not to profess it, which would not be worth it.

Youth is always stupid, even when the youth is named Rimbaud—who was indeed stupid and a genius (they are not incompatible conditions).

Sociology of fashion.— Trade must go on. The supposed sexual implications are just the excuse.

Imagine a smiling Stoic: he would be the perfect man.

For the eye to be able to see itself, it needs the mediation of a mirror. Conscience also needs one, a mirror. We do not see —or know— ourselves unless we look at ourselves in others.

«To live is to not have died yet»; «for men, to live is to await death»; etc.

A love without diappointments would not be love, it would be, what do I know, like marmalade or Bach's music.

Love still.— «S'io m'intuassi come tu inmii…»[9]. But that is impossible! First because you do not *t'emmeves*—or *t'enmies*: I cannot translate it properly—: it is I who is thinking about it.

People who, like me, are practically skeptical, we are condemned to think that what others do is right and to bear that there is always someone who finds fault in whatever we do.

Truths, they should be exaggerated so that they can be believable.

Women, like writers, are anachronical animals in essence.

It saddens me when I am listening to an intelligent person and nothing of what he says is of interest to me.

Who could stand a double of oneself?

To reflect—the very word seems to signify this—is tantamount to reflecting.[10]

Or to be reflected?

---

9 *Paradiso* IX, 81. It can be translated as "if I in-you'd me as you in-me'd you."
10 The original plays with the verbs "*reflexionar, reflectir,* and *reflectirse*", 'to reflect' and 'to be reflected'.

All philosophies are forms with many veiled—concealed even— efforts of solipsism.

We strive for centainty in everything (al least in the moral field). And I ignore why. What's the point anyway.

Not just a person's complexity of thought but also his complexity of sentimental nuances depends on the lexicon the person masters and his syntactical resources. We think and feel to the extent our language allows us.

A person that loves us is a permanent danger.

Only unexpected pleasures do not disappoint you.

Adam.— The Abominable Snowman; I mean the Paradise Man.

I would often repeat the words of that character from a novel: «Proof that I am telling the truth!». But not as a challenge but as a plea.

The more I think about it, the more I believe that being me is a form of neurosis— very uncomfortable, by the way.

Ethics for a Stranger

Repeat after me: «Nihil humani[11]...». Not even bestiality!

In every thing we do—even in what is wrong—we will only be redeemed by a great perseverance.

Accept yourself as you are. But soon after, try to make this acceptance into a remorse.

The ideas you have; the ideas that have you. The latter—and this you ignore—are the practical ones.

We should feel a trifle—if nothing else, at least a trifle— responsible for the face of our children and the fanaticism of our correligionists: in a certain manner, we are *also* guilty.

Do not be irritated: it is antihygienic.

The moralist is a man with disappointed experience of other men.

---

11 The full quote from Terence's *Heauton Timorumenos* (*The Self-Tormentor*) is "Homo sum, humani nihil a me alienum puto", which can be translated as "I am a human: I regard nothing human as foreign to me".

The innocent is not cognizant of it—which is why he is innocent.

Psychology of the confessional.—All first sins have, like Eve's, the same motive: curiosity. The second sin—the repetition of the first one—is committed out of pride. Afterwards, everything is habit.

Are you suffering? Alright: resign yourself. Nobody has been born unpunished. So said Seneca.

There are those who deserve admiration, or contempt, or indifference. And there are also those who only deserve resentment.

Are you being accused? Do not take heed. It is not fitting. Surely it is in the name of norms or myths, tacitly or explicitly, you had already abjured.

Pride always hides impotence in some way: it is the imposture of weak ones. When they talk for instance about «aristocratic pride», it must be understood that the nobles are already insecure about their class superiority. True aristocracy is a despot, a beast, but not proud.

To what extent do *the others* have the right to my sincerity?

Against good and evil—against their pretensions—we only have one defense: irony.

To live is to betray.

Here you have the most delicious face, the most beguiling smile. Well. Beneath there is a tetric and idiotic skull. We all know that. But I believe that to think about it is a veritable sin of obscenity.

And even more, all skulls—like all genders—are all the same, with minor differences.

Do not demand understading even from your best friend: at most, he will just pity you, like everybody else.

If you will consider it, you will realize that there is no one that *deserves* your envy.

Deep down inside every infatuation there is an error: without any foundation we have thought the person we loved was *someone else*.

It is good to believe that others love us; that helps us love them.

I have never admired any man of action. I regret it.

If perchance you are virtuous—whatever type of virtue you might possess—, it behooves you to conceal it. You will thus spare yourself two great nuisances: to be admired and to be scorned.

You have not chosen your life and are therefore not responsible. This is a fundamental paradox that ethical systems, if they want to admit it, cannot entirely solve.

Make certain that every misfortune of yours becomes an accusation against somebody. That will help you endure it.

Obedience is safety.

No homages, my dear! Hypocrisy is a *demand* that virtue imposes on vice.

We seldom think of the tragedy—or at least in the drama—of the hypocrite *malgré lui*[12].

Reflection for Lent.— Flesh is sad, *hélas!* Yes, it is sad, but it does not know it.

Careful! Do not ever reveal what you think you are. It is dangerous. Because others can see what you really are, and the comparison will be uncompromisingly against you.

Our neighbours' weaknesses have one advantage at least: they allow us to feel puritanical, at least for one moment.

Think—about yourself, about the world, about anything—, and you will feel different from the others: reflecting isolates you.

Heterodoxy is always loneliness.

Or viceversa: loneliness is always heterodoxy. Perhaps the choice could be: either solitary or solidary.

We frequently forget it, but it is not clear that the victims of injustice must be just themselves. Sometimes, for justice's sake, we end up defending a criminal against another criminal.

«You should experience everything», they advise me. I renounce uncomfortable experiences and idiotic experiences. That disqualifies me and limits me in many aspects, but I do not care.

Do not desert: rebel—if you can, of course.

---

12 "Despite himself".

Marriage is the only legal and honorable form of complicity recognized by our society.

The origin of gods is not just fear, as Statius[13] affirmed: it is also an instint of rebellion. Parallel to the spontaneous need to pray, there is the need to be blasphemous.

Self-gnosis.— To know yourself. That way you will become accostumed to treat yourself—*in mente* of course—so lackadaisically.

Occassionaly we feel the need to possess something, precisely so that we can lose it.

Do not wish to improvise your life: otherwise, you would run the risk of finding you are lacking «inpiration» in the most pressing moment.

It is discouraging: we all have the same flaws!

Luck is one thing—an opportunity?—of which only others *partake*.

(This principle applies to everybody.)

«Are you changing? Then it is true». To be loyal to yourself does not imply necessarily to be loyal to *your things*: to *your* ideas, *your* ethics, the concept of *your*self you have invented...

We should not fool ourselves: probity is a very expensive luxury.

Pretend to be interested in the intimate trivialities your neighbour tells you. Perhaps this way he will equally pretend to care when you tell him yours. In the end you will find that you are friends because friendship is ultimately about that.

Avarice, rather that an aberration seems to me imprudence.

Be careful not to be outraged if someone is selfish, evil or a simpleton. You are just like him. And so am I.

It is preferable to talk, to talk clearly and to say everything. The words, or half words, that remain inside will rot there.

On a different note, the real problem is: when do we have the *right* to be quiet?

---

13 *Thebaid*, III, 661.

There is he who accepts the misfortunes that befall him, as if he had brought them upon himself freely. This sort of spiritual masochism receives very respectable names.

Good faith, good faith… Fanatics, you see?, they are all people of good faith.

Above all the other things that are repugnant about prostitution, the essential one is that it constitutes a bitterly blatant form of simony.

Kill time… This expression encapsulates a full program: it offers us time as the enemy. And perhaps there is no other way to salvation.

Sometimes we must be evil out of compassion.

Precisely because the world is unjust, or imperfect—as you choose—, man needs hope to live. It is true though that it is just a way of deceiving the body: but it can console, or be the cause of rebellion—which is another form of consolation.

There is nothing more healthy from a moral standpoint than to make clear the part of truth we will not be able to snatch from our enemies.

Not everybody is capable of getting bored. Boredom indeed requires a refined technique and a very particular personal predisposition. In essence, one must have much imagination, exhaust it and then long for it.

Narcissus was an idler. When one does not have anything to do, one has a tendency to look at oneself. And after so much self-contemplation, one finds himseld admirable, handsome and even very dignified. The rest of the myth is equally terrible.

To love thy enemy. Alright. But it would be ideal to be able to love him without considering him an enemy.

We aren't only what we propose ourselves to be.

We look frequently after success, whatever form of success, even the most absurd type, because we have not been able to attain happiness.

There is no authentic love without some vileness in its most delicate aspects.

«Clara cum laude notitia»[14]: that is human glory, according to St. Thomas Aquinas.

---

14 "Brilliant notoriety with praise", that is glory according to St. Augustine, as quoted by St. Thomas Aquinas in *Summa contra gentiles*.

Most clearly, to dwell on it is not worth it.

Very often, people avoid doing something by alleging disdain or modesty. But do not be fooled! Under these protestations, there is on many occassions pure and simple impotence.

Hypothetically speaking, to the most noble and uninterested actions we can always attribute one or another form of infamous motivation. In most cases, this motivation is even present.

Do not hope nor fear, and you will be perfect.

A dialectical injunction.— Scream when you debate and you will be right. Generally, he who is wrong also screams. You are not going to lose your stance because of politeness.

Well understood charity begins with yourself; so does hatred.

It would be unjust to reproach Galileo for recanting his scientific assertions in order to save his life. In the end, a truth—if it is really a truth—continues being the truth whether one dies for it or not, and from an intellectual standpoint a martyr is never an argument. But still, for Galileo his own life had to be more *dear* than any truth whatsoever.

Nowadays adultery is corny.

Who can really recant something they have said? When it is convenient to us, we recant our words; but that is only an appearance.

The art of avoiding inconsistency.— Instead of adopting some principles and to subject our behavior to them, it is preferable to deduce the principles from the behavior we follow. Perhaps in this case they won't be very eminent principles, but this is also an advantage.

One only feels truly alone when one does not have anything to think about—or when one is afraid to think about something.

To criticize others is not a vice as shameful as they say. While you engage in it, you do not fall into the temptation of criticizing yourself, which would be a worse vice..

It is the youth's duty to scare old people, even if only to prevent them from falling asleep permanently.

Refuse, in principle, everything defined as ineffable, or mysterious, or merely esoteric. At night, all cows are black.

Think about *something else*, and you will find peace.

In general, it is not our prejudices that oblige us to behave in this or that manner; upon further examination, it is others' prejudices that do this.

Some defects are so deeply rooted and we feel them as such a part of us, that we do not enjoy changing them because we do not want them to become virtues. And in the end, who knows if virtues are all the same.

Only with death can you be free of yourself. Resign yourself, then, to not being free *ever*.

What really makes us melancholic is not so much a longing for the past as it is a withdrawl from the future—and in practice it is not easy for us to distinguish one from another.

Do not advise anyone to stop doing something if you have not done it before, nor advise them to do something if you have done it. In fact, however little you can, do not give any advice ever.

Two siblings are never more united—they never feel more *siblings*—than when they team up against their father.

There are moments when you feel inferior to yourself. What a subtle and twisted form of vanity!

We do many things only so that we can talk about them. Robinson was virtuous, but not because he lacked occassions but because he lacked partners with whom to chat or in whom to confide.

«Nihil humani…», still.— Respectable people are ultimately those who find that there are human things—some things—that are strange to them.

An assassin is also an instrument of Nature's designs and forces.

Believe me, young one: do not pay attention! At your age, one spends his life tricking himself.

Measure every man by their most unworthy action, but treat them with the regard due to their most noble deeds; and let it be on record: this is not duplicity, but realism and sense of humor.

Clov.—Do you believe in future life?

Hamm.—La mienne l'a toujours été.¹⁵ (S. Beckett, Fin de partie.) It is useful to always have one or other obsession: it will serve as a distraction.

Life will deny everything to you but it will always provide you with an opportunity: that of desperately mocking others, and mocking them rightfully.

«The wounds of a friend are faithful; the kisses of an enemy are perfidious»¹⁶, we read in the Bible. But we—everybody—abhor blows and are moved by kisses. And upon further reflection, blows are not the most plausible sign of friendship.

In this world, it seems that everybody is honorable until they no longer are.

If there is sin, everything is sin.

(Even Theology itself—or especially—: to use the name of God in vain)

We only act reasonably by instinct. Most decisions adopted consciously, thoroughly and with great lucidity are usually insane and stupid.

—And you, who do not have nor hope for anything, what do you live for?

—In order not to die.

We must be on time for everything: love, success, misfortune, death. Hastiness or an insignificant delay can thwart your success.

Even with the most sensual pleasures there is an intelligent way to enjoy them.

Every setback is a warning: you do not have the *right* to expect what you are hoping for.

To have yourself killed—for whatever reason: a crime, an ideal, a passion—is still a manner of suicide and it shouldn't be whitewashed.

Granted that you want to talk about it…— *Sacra sacre tractanda*¹⁷. That is, with silence.

Happiness, as the men of the Portico assured us, consists in not desiring: in not feeling any desire, I would add. Lack of appetite is a state of perfection, perhaps the only one.

Playing is always losing—at the very least, time.

---

15 "Mine has existed always".
16 Ps. 27:6.
17 "Sacred matters must be treated sacredly".

For good or bad—generally for good—each of our acts is but a rough parody of our intentions.

Paternity induces idiocy.

Geese have always had beaks. Historical periods that one usually qualifies as deeply depraved only surpass the others in one depravity: frankness.

The sense of responsibility is the only useful form of fear I know.

Truth does not always agree with justice, I must caution you. Only not very sensual people can be fully materialistic without great effort.

I am still convinced that all dilemmas are false: traps to make you do or accept something that repulses you.

Pain is only egregious and repulsive when it seems useless to us. In any case, whoever suffers it thinks that it is *always* useless.

Works and Days

Writing—literature—is everything you say and additionally it is a form of vengeance.

One of the dangers the artist is exposed to is that of becoming a *precursor*. That means being an epigone who was born before his due time.

Disabuse yourselves, my friends who are concert-goers: music—all music, from Palestrina or Bach to Armstrong or Stravinski—is to be danced to or to be sang.

Piero della Francesca would have been an ingeniously perfect painter had he been able to paint a smile.

Claudel is Victor Hugo, but worse and orthodox.

Each word is already, in itself, a periphrasis.

Some of Josep Carner's ironies provoke in me the effect that he, the poet, has the tired elegance of he who «has read all books» and nonetheless finds amusing— *only* finds amusing—to write more on his part.

I have not known yet an enthusiastic reader of Nietzsche—and they do exist!— that is not, as a person, a ridiculous character.

The worst thing about plagiarism is not that it is a theft, rather that it is redundant.

We must recognize it: «to admire»—that is, to feel admiration for someone or something—is a very tiring operation and in the long-run, soporific.

The opposite of a good painter (or a bad painter) is not a bad painter (or a good painter), but rather Picasso.

Literature is a petit-bourgeois prejudice.

(Josep M. Castellet, to whom I have said this, replies that this is precisely a petit'bourgeois idea. Perhaps, and then, even more in my favor.)

In art, as in any other activity, it behooves you to imitate as long as you can. Only when there is no other remedy it is tolerable to be original.

The absurd, old and uncatalogued muse...

The most contemptible and repulsive literary genres can be ingeniously illustrated. In fact, Shakespeare did it with melodrama; Dostoevsky with *folletin*; Hegel with philosophy; the «absurd» by Aristophanes.

Advice to myself.— Let every one of your words be, at least, a reticence.

Vivaldi's music is pure conversation.

The great artist is all his life is an industrious student of himself.

André Gide's secret is that he made his puberty last until he was eighty years old.

If the autor of Ecclesiastes had truly been as pessimistic as he claims, he would not have written his book.

The death of the Goethe follower.— They say Thomas Mann's last words were: «Where are my glasses?». Practically, the sentence equals the entire «light, more light!». (August, 1955.)

Joan Miró has a likeness to the Holy Spirit.

(Or: If the Holy Spirit painted, he would do it like Joan Miró.)

There is a group of writers that could be defined as «gentlemen who have never read Plato». For instance, Pío Baroja.

Liszt: A sacred orator..

In every novel, half of it is superfluous.

Franz Kafka's works tend to be what we used to refer to as «philosophical narratives». Although it may seem very strange, it is similar to Swift, and Voltaire, and *Don Quixote*, and some contemporary novels, such as *Brave New*

World. By this we understand that Kafka's "philosophical narratives" have at the end, not a philosophy, but a devastation.

Does the poet really say what I understand when I read it? It does not matter.

It is enough that I *understand* something. If it is not what the poet said, it is what I was about to tell myself.

Eugeni d'Ors? Yes, of course. That old right-wing French intellectual!

About literary style.— Simplicity is not always compatible with precision.

Mozart's great superiority lies in the fact that he is *still* an Italian musician.

«…aboli bibelot d'inanité sonore[18]…».— Couldn't it be that deep down abstract painting is pure plastic inanity?

As a general rule, modern Catalan literature is done by satisfied, sedentary and undeceived husbands, as well as by chaplains. This is why it is clearly enchanting and especially repetitive.

The truth is that jazz, with its imitations and derivativations, has made us all in the end a little mulattos.

With all due respect, Marcel Proust seems to me the exact replica, in literature, of chewing gum—that is, of bubble-gum.

Adjectives are always subjective.
Shakespeare.— The best passage from *Romeo and Juliet* is Tchaikovsky's overture.

And who knows if Romeo's destiny in the end was to be a cuckold!

To describe is to inventory: a subordinate activity characteristic of notaries or painful novelists.

Be wary of those who criticize Descartes! They will end up selling Pascal to you, and you already know what that means.

An adjective for Bosco's painting: fraudulent.

There are literary styles compatible with the typewriter.

Provided a more or less suggestive vocabulary, philosophy is *almost* a syntactical matter, just like poetry is *almost* a prosodic question.

---

18 "Abolished trinket of inane sonority" (Mallarmé, *Poésies*, Sonnet allégorique de lui-même).

In the end, to value culture by its utility will be—considering how things are turning—the only way to save it.

We write with our enemies in mind: either to proselytize or to corrupt them.

Rameau's hapsichord has a toothache.

Whatever contemporary painters may say, as well as critics, the crucial aspect of a portrait is its likeness; physical similarity. But it is also true that this similarity is only of interest to the sitter and their closest family members.

I greatly admire the work of Salvador Espriu, among other more serious reasons because he has interspersed a bit of semitism amidst a literature with so much Hellenistic pretensions as the Catalan literature of the Noucentism.

Someone has remarked that no statue has ever been dedicated to a critic. Perhaps that is one reason why critics strengthen their vocation.

Joyce.— *Ulysses* could only have been written by a devout pervert, an ex-student of a religious school.

Mauriac says that the goal of the novel is "to know men". And I think, at best to know the man who writes.

It is surprising how many stupidities they say on our behalf—and what is worse, with a clear conscience—, quoting us as an illustrious author.

Topic of musical aesthetics.— To find out whether the flat is as expressive of pain as Schopenhauer affirmed, or if on the contrary it does not express more than pain, hunger, or the categorical imperative.

I think the poetry that should be done nowadays should be one motivated by wrath or sarcasm. Or simply just by wrath: because deep down sarcasm is but wrath attenuated by insidiousness.

Montaigne.—He said, when referring to his writings: «Mes songes que voici[19]...». Wouldn't it be better: «Mensonges que voici...»? Just like Montaigne, everybody else. To write is to do comedy.

Preferences.— Picasso or reality. Miró or happiness. Klee or silence. Chagall or truth.

---

19 Play on words between mes *songes*, songs, and *mensonges*, lies.

If you are capable of reading large quantities of Huxley, you will end up imagining him as an awe-inspiring, incessant, prodigal, miraculous and useless thinking machine.

The ill of Wagner is that we inevitably see him as a liar.

Mr. Navarro Costabella said—or they say he said—that the greatest known novelist was Tolstoievsky: but that depends on how you look at it, because he could also be the worst.

We have invented archaeology and must suffer the consequences: I mean, we will be their topic in the future.

With good feelings one makes bad literature; with wicked feelings, also. In general, bad is literatura is made, above all with feelings.

It is incredible how many stupidities Baudelaire wrote in verse. We could not have possibly believed it!

Believe me, as a heart-felt recommendation. Read Bertrand Russell. He is not a philosopher, he is a disinfectant.

The truth is: Fortuny is a great painter, Salvador Dalí is not.

You already know this: in poetry, there are theories based on inspiration and others that give priority to deliberation. There are good *inspired* poets and good *deliberate* poets. Nonetheless, looking at it carefully, inspiration is just a deliberation, but so quickly and mysteriously done that it almost does not seem a deliberation.

There is only one serious way to read, which is to reread.

Music, what you call music, purebred music, that is Mozart, Chopin, Ravel, Corelli, Tchaikovsky, Telemann, Vivaldi, and even Mendelsohn: but not Bach, nor Beethoven, nor Wagner, nor Debussy, nor Stravinsky.

Curious: Plato was a great reader of Aristophanes. One finds some of the works by the lewd playwright under the pillow, in the death bed of the philosopher. It is a pity that Kant, Hegel, Heidegger did not have the same literary preference.

Risk of literary interpretation.— The critic can end up believeing that the work he is analyzing has been written exclusively for him to exercise his role as commentator.

It is likely, in fact, that Picasso has entered his decadence, as some critics affirm. Who could be shocked? It is a right the old painter had well earned.

Walt Whitman had the virtue of not seeing the coarseness of coarse things. That is why he could write a song to himself, to the crowds, to his country.

No: the good bourgeois *gentilhomme* did not have any reason to be surprised. He did not speak in prose. Nobody speaks in prose without knowing it, that is without knowing about it. In reality, only the lecturers speak in prose.

I have not been able to hear the final chords of the ninth symphony as if they were music, but as what they really are, an anthem. Now: I am not very sure that it has ever felt to me as an ode to joy—rather something else, I do not know, but more noble.

Neo-scholasticism.— Maritain—Maritain and the others—reminds me of that recommendation in the Gospels, do not patch a piece of new cloth onto an old dress, because you lose the piece, the dress and ultimately your time.

Books do not *substitute* life, but life does not substitute books either. All verses are already written. In this case, we are referring to poetry.

Look at this beautiful countenance of Nefertiti, or Michelangelo's David or Mrs. Cayetana's inappropriate body. Where is, oh Death, your victory?

Goethe is hateful—like a mountain or like a downpour.

It is difficult to distinguish in Dostoyevsky where Christianity ends and where the consequences of epilepsy begin (or viceversa).

From some points of view *Das Kapital*—so to speak—is also escape literature: everything depends on what you want to escape from.

A happy man does not feel the need to express himself.

The verses that proclaim a happy love have been written always *after*, already in a moment of boredom or desperation—and with the intention of solving them.

When Stendhal fortold that his work would be understood by 1890

—year more, year less—, he well could have added that it would stop being understood by 1990.

As a detractor of the modern world and its supposed aberrations, Papini—that is the Papini of *Gog* and *Il libro nero*—gives the impression of a small luxury dog: mischievous, noisy, barking without biting, and above all he tires you with his useless and dizzying games.

In reality, if well considered, it becomes clear that the important poets have always limited themselves to writing verses to the moon.

In Rodin's nudes, one can discern that the clothes the figures have just taken off themselves are the shaming and industrial robes of the 19th century: there is, on the sculpted surface, the imprint of a cheap undergarment.

Poe—he said so himself—was artificial by nature. Most of us, poor people!, attempt to be, or to seem, natural artificially.

Renan.— A nun. Incredulous and erudite, though.

(I am wondering how can I have wasted even one hour reading him.)

Metaphors—good metaphors—are but unexpected definitions: to say the same thing, but unexpectedly. It is a way of disguising their triviliaty, and for this reason poets use them copiously.

D'Annunzio was, in my opinion, the fakest character of his own literature. Which is quite something!

Perhaps it would be excessive to say that New Orleans anonymous musicians come directly from Frescobaldi or Pergolesi; but you will grant me, at least, that Cole Porter and Irving Berlin are Puccini's sons.

The first obligation of a writer is to make himself be read.

A statistical analysis, quite accurate, based on the total volume of Catalan literature produced from the "Renaixença" onwards, demonstrates that, with regard to its tòpics:

> *a)* 60% is a more or less academic gloss of Verdaguer's verses that say:
> Tot sia per vós,
> Jesuset
> dolcíssim; tot
> sia per vós,
> Jesús amorós[20];
>
> *b)* 30% deals with the Empordà; and

---

20 "May everything be for your sake, / sweetest / Jesus; everything / may be for your sake, / loveliest Jesus".

c) the remaining 10% deals with the topics that are to be expected in any civilized literature.

Imitating Goethe.— There is nothing *sublime* that, expressed in a certain manner, does not seem humorous.

Sade, Maldoror and C^a., they have never really interested me. Systematic monstrosity seems to me very easy and dull.

For some painters, the worse they paint, the greater they are. Example: the Goya of the Black Paintings. But this phenomenon only occurs, to begin with, when they are already great painters.

I am very envious of Carles Riba, if, in reality, he is as happy as he claims in his verses.(1951)

Reading little turns you away from life; reading much makes you close to it.

«Life is short and art seems long...», translated Ausiàs. Thus, the saying «make haste slowly[21]» is inadvisable. Rather: either make haste or give it up.

There are enervating pianos: Debussy's is one of those, for instance.

The greatest 20th-century Spanish poets are Latin American: one, of course, Pablo Neruda; the other, that gentleman, I cannot remember now,—with an Italian last name, I believe—, who wrote the lyrics for Carlos Gardel's tangos.

Expressed in a different manner.— the History of Philosophy is a chapter of the History of Literature where we put the great unreadable books.

It seems that there are many types of Romanticism. Henry Miller, for instance, is a romantic: a sort of romantic Aretinus—a sad and anarchical Aretinus. Not all romantics are romantics at heart: some are romantics according to their hypogastrium.

«Was bleibet aber, stiften es die Dichter». Which means—as they say—: \«Whatever lasts has been founded by poets». Naturally, it is a poet who said it.

General rule.— «Sometimes Zapata contradicts himself, as do all those writers called *essayists*...» (M. Menéndez Pelayo, *Orígenes de la novela*, cap. IX).

I do not why, but Mendelssohn's concert for violin makes think of Shelly.

Paul valéry.—Yes, yes, whatever you want. But diamonds are not edible.

---

21 Two well-known Renaissance emblems: *Ars longa, vita brevis; Festina lente.*

After reading Lukács, one gets the impression that it is very difficult to produce literature without playing into the hands of capitalism. And the bad thing is that it is true.

For a writer, bile can be a good stylistic ingredient.

For One, For Many

Quis custodiet ipsos custodes? That is the question! Et tout le reste est littérature[22]...

«To be in charge» equals «to despise». (And, in addition, he who pays, is in charge)

Only if you see history as a permanent expiation, it will stop seeming absurd and criminal to you. But then, obviously, so will seem the expiation itself.

If crowds are wild, violent, and blind it is because they are composed of individuals who are, approximately, just like us.

«Ideas do not come from fists». That is evident. But our ideas are different after receiving some blows. Especially if we are the one receiving them.

France.— In reality, nowadays the *Marsellaise* is nothing but monsieur Chauvin's aphrodisiac.

In any case, there is a considerable advantage in considering work as a punishment rather than a merchandise.

On many ocasions, you must have heard principle according to which «the end does not justify the means». But look who is saying it. You will see that in most cases it is a gentleman settled in his seat who does not want to remember how he got there and wants even less to be removed.

When King Faruk of Egypt was dethroned, a traveling salesman told me quite accurately:

—To be king, nowadays, is a mistake.

Wars, hunger, oppressions.... The common crimes of our society are as monstruous as they are freqüent. But the greatest of all, is to have become accustomed to the point that our indifference makes us complicit.

---

22 "Who watches over the watchman"; "The rest is trivial".

«The proprietor, that prehistoric animal». Truly!

Great lovers—those who deserve the honor of poetry or annals (Romeo and Juliet, Paolo and Francesca, Hero and Leander, Aga Khan and his wives, etc.)—are typically affluent people. Love is a rich person's exercise: at least an exercise for idle people.

He who has a tongue, comes from Rome.

Cogito ergo sumus[23]. What will we do!

There are two types of christians—two ways of professing any ideology—: those who choose to remember that «he that is not with me is against me» (Math., xii, 12: 30), and those who believe that «whoever is not against us is for us» (Luc., ix, 9: 50).

The most tempting aspect of revolutions is that one does not know where they will take you.

The sins—or vices—condemned by traditional ethics are not gratuitous: pay attention and you will see how all of them turn out to be socially anti-economic.

Justice is the most corrosive idea invented by men. With it we enjoy opposing God, revolutionizing society and killing our neighbors. But we must remember that without it, indeed, we would be just a sadly abject victim.

The history of Italy is a beautiful opera: what tenors!, what elevators!, what scenery!, what hearts!

In every moment in history, all «lost causes» are so because of the same—deep—reason, and that unites them. The day their supporters realize it, their causes begin to be achievable, if not already achieved.

A prophet provokes rather than foresees.

A prophet is a man who is outraged. That is why only catastrophes are prophesied.

«Jerusalem, Jerusalem…».— Let us imagine that People did not stone their prophets. What would happen?

On the other hand, history only remembers the prophets who got it right.

---

23 "I think, therefore we are".

On the destiny of western civilization and etc.— I do not know why. Probably because I have reached a large degree of saturation: saturation of…, of everything, I cannot be specific. The truth is that I am overtaken by a violent need to write a poem that begins in this manner:

>Oh, Lord, send us already
>The Barbarians. Do not make us
>deserve them more!

Mutatis mutandis.— Fear the man with only one newspaper (St. Augustin).

Europe's ill is that there are still millions of Jacobins to be civilized.

The slave rarely revolts. A man sunk in misery, in the *most* abject misery, tends towards suicide or resignation. Revolution, particularly social revolution, occurs when the oppressed stop being so. That is: when the oppressor has yielded slightly due to negligence or kindness.

Perhaps what is most repulsive about the actions of the dominant peoples, is the fact of imposing on the the subordinate peoples their insoluble mediocrity. Rome's case is not the only one.

Directed literature.— Because «we cannot prevent a bird from singing», it is advisable to teach him solfa.

Naturally, this gentleman that screams and protests, outraged, against demagogy is not part of the *demos*.

Cinema has been frequently termed as «art for the masses». It would be better to say «art against the masses». All contemporary tyrannies—*nec nominetur*[24]— have profited from the stupefying power of cinema to dull the social and human sensibility of audiences. Capitalistic cinema is precisely the opium of the people. Propaganda cinema is another form of opium: with the same numbing effect but without amusing dreams.

Violence begets violence. But do not forget—tolerance also begets violence, and hopelessness begets violence, and—above all—truth begets violence.

Antigone's mistake was to forget that, in the last moment, Gods side with the established powers.

---

24 Let us not mention any. This is a clear reference to Franco´s regime.

Totalitarian state? Isn't that a tautology?

Religious persecutions, in some countries, have a hint of a crime of passion: «I killed her because she was mine»...

Technique.— «Oh! More than one organ of death was born out of a quiet calculation...» You are so right, Mr. Rilke!

It is good to discredit heroism, because a hero is always a dangerous beast and a demoralizing example. But it could also be dangerous to shed our heroic models. As long as the enemy does not do the same—*not disheroizing*—, it will behoove us to cultivate our own heroes. At least to be able to make them face the opposing heroes when the moment of truth comes.

I do not know why we put a derogatory meaning on the words *plebs* and *plebeian*. I am a plebeian, but do not consider myself despicable in the least.

On the historical origin of the strike.— One, in Greece. Aristophanes records it in *Lysistrata*. It was a gender strike.

«Salus ex judaeis est[25]». Perhaps they said it because of Marx.

As could be inferred from what expert observers say, English people used to be a caricature of an Englishman.

It seems strange to me that many of those who praise or admire Napoleon, despise and blame Ramon Cabrera. After all, as human beings—not as supporters of ideologies nor as technicians of strategies, of course—, I cannot find any difference between them except from an important one: that Napoleon killed more people (or had them killed).

The day that we take stock of the merits of resentment, we will see that they are not insignificant. With resentment we would not have Revolution, Nationalism, nor the best part of the *Divine Comedy*.

Laws are made by those who are in a position to respect them—and exclusively *because* they are there.

In addition, all laws have the same goal: to protect trading—which explains everything.

«Don Quijote, Don Juan, Don Myself...».

---

25 "Salvation is from the Jews" (John 4:22).

Yes, madam! «Your devoted and attentive servant, who kisses the hands of your mercy, Pepe».

It was necessary to invent these nuclear bombs. For a long time humankind had already lost one of the oldest habits of Christian civilization, the belief in the immediate end of the world; now we can resume it.

«Engagée» literature.— I get the impression that whenever literature is not resentful, then it is complacent.

Illustrious dogmatics assume that human knees are only made, or mostly made, for kneeling. As expected, several political and religious doctrines are derived from this assumption.

A politician is an opportunist or he is not a politician.

In war, in all sort of struggles, each side tries to do what they think the other side would do in the same circumstances. These assumptions, of course, are eminently reprehensible. We calm down, though, when we think that—to use a popular expression—«it is not a sin to do as they do». But this, in fact, equals a simple and secret «to do as I do ».

Everybody is liberal *to a certain degree*, and I do not know any anarchist who is just an anarchist *to a certain degree*.

I am not sure if Europeans are the gradfathers of Americans or if rather we will be their grandchildren.

The great happiness of the bourgeois is that he is a bourgeois without realizing it.

«Wrapped up in rags, she despises what she ignores», said Antonio Machado about Castile.

«They used to laugh about what they do not understand», said Joan Maragall about Catalans.

One ill for another, I do not know which one is worse. With the exception of *rags*, of course.

The true end of a war is not the peace that follows but another war.

In property and in love—which is a form of property—, it is essential not to enjoy the property of the object of love as much as to prevent someone else from enjoying it.

(We could also say: «In love and in property—which is a form of love—, it is essential…, etc.»).

He who is ready to die for an ideal, is deep down also ready to kill for that ideal. All doctrines that begin with martyrs end up with an inquisition.

Nobody demands freedom but to show themselves ruthless in one way or another.

There have always. been tyrannies; it is almost certain that there will always be some. The most bearable ones are those that are not being exercised under the name of high principles.

The only genuine and positive politics are the stupidly defamed «bell tower politics»: that of small problems and small passions. The other type of politics—high politics—is just fantasy: rhetoric and adventure, half and half; catastrophic quite frequently, or useless in the best cases.

We should encourage conscientious objection, not only against war but also—and particularly—against some forms of peace.

It is good to feel linked to a tribe: it is a way to have deceased, gods, and children without the need of making them yourself.

Looking at History, one gets the feeling that Germans have waged war—and so many of them!—just for the pleasure of seeing themselves defeated.

«It is as difficult for the rich to become a sage as it is for the sage to acquire wealth». So said Epictetus, who was poor—a slave—and, obviously, a sage. Because in this world, if one does not find consolation it is only because one does not want to.

The inhabitants of the Iberian Peninsula, when things are not working, accuse themselves of being individualistic and they think that that explains everything.

Leisure is basically harmful. The day that machines, automated or more productive, offer men almost unlimited free time—everything is possible—, havoc will be wrecked. For instance, people's tendency towards alcohol, philosophy and suicide will be more abundant.

The myth of the *bon sauvage*[26] was not that silly: civilized man feels a bit sinister in front of his own conscience.

---

26 "Good savage".

History teaches us that the only defect of periods of terror—the French Revolution and so many others—is that, considering subsequent development, they were always *insufficient*: short-lived and lacking intensity.

When Russians have learned to add, the charm of the «Slavic soul» will quickly fade away.

Idea of a nation.— The old Latin saying, utilitarian and serious, says: «Ubi bene, ibi patria». Huysmans, spiritual and pious, says: «Ma patrie c'est où je prie bien[27]». Ultimately, both attitudes are equivalent.

Society cannot be deceived. It knows that madness is just a biological excuse for certain forms of noncomformity. A mental asylum, as well as a hospital, functions as a prison.

It is logical that every Marxist is more Marxist than Marx himself.

«Summum ius, summa iniuria[28]». But you do not have to reach a «summum». Every *ius* is already an *iniuria*, in some social conditions—for instance, ours.

People from all races typically coincide on this front—including Jews—: their hatred toward Jews.

(Maybe I am exaggerating, but not much.)

Under equal conditions, they say—I do not understand—, the same causes produce the same effects. Probably. but not in history, in which the effects are worse each time.

We should mistrust those who predicate the idea of sacrifice: that means they need someone to sacrifice *for them*.

Comedy passage.

> First character:.—«Dieu et mon droit[29]!»
> Second character.—What do you say?
> Third character.—God and the right of this gentleman.
> Second character.—Ah!

A weakling—no matter his weakness—is always a delinquent: jurists ratify it.

---

27 "Home is where it's good"; "Home is where I pray well".
28 "The greatest right is the greatest injustice".
29 "God and my right", a monarchs's divine right to rule in the *Ancien Régime*.

To be persecuted is already a victory.

Every people, so say the Scriptures, has its sage and its madman (or—*and* or—its idiot). And also its righteous one and its villain. Without them, of course, *the rest* perhaps could not consider themselves people—*a* people.

We believe that, whenever a crime *is necessary* for whatever reason, ipso facto it is not a *crime* any more. And that is, evidently, a sinister contradiction. A necessary crime is still a crime and must be assumed as such.

Take advantage of the first occasion that arises to become accusers before the others do so: with it you have already won half the game.

When taken literally, it is dangerous to follow the advice of letting the dead bury their dead. The «deceased» do not care. And, when neither are buried, both stink... or make us believe that they are still alive, and that further complicates the matter.

Rulers, naturally, lie because of fear.

Enthusiam? It does not help to build a house, nor to write a book or plough a field, not even to play soccer. With enthusiasm one can only sing—and badly at that.

For the poor, money is a mystery. That is why they continue being poor.

Everywhere there should exist the possibility of founding a political party that has as its sole purpose the opposition to the foolishness of the other parties.

It seems strange that man has taken so long to invent museums, very comfortable armchairs, tango, sociology, vacations—and so many other things that have nothing to do with scientific progress. Perhaps we are not as intelligent animals as we would like ourselves to believe.

Thalassa! Thalassa[30]*!...* Yes, but from the shore.

Nation—also—means war: *id est*, trade as much as accolades and cemeteries.

You can only create culture during coffee time; that is, after having eaten. Could someone who is moderately starving be interested in the problem of *analogia entis*, the prosodical particularities of Dante, quantum theory, or even the concept of capital gain?

---

30 "The sea, the sea". From Greek Θάλασσα. The quote comes from Xenophon, *Anabasis*.

It is incomprehensible that by singing the «Carmagnole» and the «Ça ira», the French of '93 could have revolted: they seem rather like local tavern songs for Easter. Or perhaps it is not true that «le ton qui fait la chanson»?

«Success is a justification», Napoleon said. So is failure. Or neither of them justify anything. Or (even) nothing can be justified.

All flags are equally insidious. Standard-bearers are more trustworthy than colors.

Force is also a means of persuasion. Notwithstanding: the slowest and most fragile of which we know. In general, there are few people willing to be persuaded by anything: not even by force.

Do not deceive yourselves: power changes hands, but seldom hesitates.

Pessimists, of course, come from the right. Indeed, what is there to fear, by he who has nothing to lose?

(But sometimes I think: who is not conservative—atleast separated in one aspect or other?)

General Absolution and Plenary Indulgence

And in the end, what? We must die. There is no other solution. Let it be, then.

Good morning, my reader friend, future corpse, future nothing! *Sit tibi terra levis*[31]*!*

---

31 "May the earth rest lightly on you", a typical Latin epitaph.

Indecent Proposals[32]

Initial Caution

«Proposals», yes, but with the meaning of «utterance of a thought», to use Fabra's style.

And every «proposition», shouldn't it also be a «purpose» and a «proposal»?

I have always believed that «honesty» is a concept stipulated by others.

Randomly Observed

There are useful impostures. Geometry, for instance.

Regardless of their literal meaning, interjections always seem to be casting a spell.

Life, alas!, it is so fragmentary!

Where there is much light, everything seems a little obscene.
Boredom endorses everything. A bored man is capable of doing anything dauntlessly.

We say: «fixed idea». But then it is not an idea.

You need great health to be passionate.

The most difficult body part to convince is the genitalia. Or the easiest—it depends on how you look at it.

True crimes are secret.

Sometimes, recklessness engenders good results.

Love is not a question of Love, but of skill.

---

32 The title, *proposals*, can be interpreted as the plural of transgressing or heterodox statements, while *indecent proposals* can be understood as well as referring to the idea of sexual/erotic dishonesty or sexual predation. In the prologue to this volume, Vicent Salvador indicates that it points to the ideas of illicitness and transgression.

Whoever seems to make concessions—a young lady, a politician, a salesman—, is only after demands.

Only ignorance is consoling.

In fact, dogs practice adulation rather than loyalty.

Appearances do not deceive, they are appearances.

The most noxious parasites we can handle are our critics.

Everything depends on the word.

Man has invented man, and for this reason it is a man or seems to be one. (Variant or recitfication: Man has created man in his own image. Patience!)

Only he that does not hope, is truly ambitious.

Nothing unites us more than shared madness.

Elegance is expensive—even what they call «natural elegance».

From a certain point of view, we constantly arrive late everywhere.

Nowadays, sighing is obsolete.

The most painful loss is that of what we haven't had yet.

Women live; men, in general, think they live.

A hostile will, we usually call «a mistake». It is a rash identification.

Some are stupid out of pure laziness.

Mistrusting people are right in mistrusting, but they almost never mistrust as much as they should.

Living is unhygienic.

Good customs also corrupt.

It is precisely because we are carnivors, that we need veterinarians.

Sometimes, obstinacy can be mistaken as a creed, an ideal, or a theory. There are people who live just inside stubbornness.

Roses are immortal, don't you think? Our hands are always empty.

Indifference is mostly diurnal.

Irritable temperaments tend towards austerity, fanaticism, and—beware!—treason.

We are sincere inasmuch as it is convenient for us, and no more.

Ultimately, life seems so improbable to us, that we have been incapable of imagining it.

It is a pity, but 2 plus 2 are not 4, except on paper, and even so it is not for sure. Perhaps on paper, to say that 2 plus 2 are 4 is nothing more than a pleonasm.

Everything requires training. Even pain.

Humanism.— Man would never have «invented» the sea.

...The dramatically serious basis of all tackiness...

A failure cannot be improvised.

Women are men who are so alienated that they are not even women.

Sleeping is also waiting.

The word *snob*, does it not already seem archaic?

Nobody can live without victimizing someone. Or without victimizing themselves.

When someone appoints themself as the judge of their brother, it is because they have already decided to find him guilty.

Some people fight when they make love.

Happiness... Happiness, let us be clear, consists of any form of abuse.

In some situations, silence becomes the most infamous resource of defamation.

There is no merit in dying at night.

Fatigue induces incredulity.

One needs to be slightly cynical to decide to protect animals and plants.

People say: «To do as they do is not a sin». That is: «The more the merrier».

There are men who deserve to be cuckolded. If they are not, it is their wive's fault.

Verbal excesses are usually frivolous. To utter a good insult, a worthy insult, one must be cold-blooded.

In the long term, good reputations are not beneficial at all.

There are almost no misanthropes nowadays. Bad sign.

And chastity, what about it? Is it not a form of avarice?

Ultimately, we are what others let us be, and frequentlym what others want us to be.

Happiness is never innocent.

They say rage is blind. A lucid rage: that would be ideal.

We live by dint of great patience. But we do not realize that it is, preceisely, patience.

A husband always cuts a comic figure.

«Deception» consists of making someone believe precisely what they want to believe in.

All our actions are incomplete.

Luxury is a form of deception.

The faces we make while sleeping are involuntary. It should not be taken into account.

Nobody confesses it openly, but bidets are the totems of our times.

We tend to be very indulgent with our flaws, and that is, upon close inspection, the weakness most worth forgiving.

When we are in the dark, we turn the light on, and we refer to it as «Light».

Vinegar is still wine.

A disappointed fanatic closely resembles a skeptic. But pay attention!

There are praises that are true aggressions.

Family is also a matter of talent.

The idea of a driver in distress— When God sleeps, machines break down.

Adulthood is reached when the son feels compassion for his father. Despite what the law says.

At the time of death, everybody owes a rooster to one Asclepius or other.

Ideas for Family Children

When we say «I have the right», we have already cheated.

Unfortunately, scratching us when it's not itching is good for nothing.

Deep down, love is just a venereal disease like any other.

Happy people lack memory.

Teeth are for biting, in principle. It is unnatural to show them when smiling.

At the rate the world is going, the day will come when being young will be a merit.

And sleepiness, isn't it a vice?

Upon closer inspection, the act of lying already forces us to consider the truth.

Your brother doubts you, and so do your wife and your father. It is natural, isn't it?

Any excess has the virtue of warning us that it is, precisely, an *excess*.

It is deliberate, ergo unforgivable.

Strength is never innocent. Not even the strength of an athlete.

To express a passion is tantamount to reducing it by half.

Misfortunes can also be ridiculous.

Despite our best efforts, we will never be as stupid as we desire. We are sentimental out of frivolity.

There are occassions in which what seems to be an adversity is nothing more than a simple misunderstanding.

Between lovers, jealousy can only be justified with self-defense.

If you promise, you already allow it.

Money is nothing more than a conjecture. The unforeseen is disturbing.

Forgetful people always have a clear conscience.

Under certain circumstances, to slander is to tell the truth, or at least, to fabricate it.

Blessed are the timid, because they will refrain themselves.

Solitude is tiring; so is company. There is no solution.

Luck falls on those who already have it.

At the core of every voluptuosity, there usually lies a sophism.

He who understands, does not admire.

Past happiness is, in general, a bitter memory. Dante said this already. But we want it to be so.

Among other things, a mistake is a lack of education.

Quite frequently, we must fulfill our duties without loyalty. They call this an «affront to virtue», but it is just life.

And who does not have a desertor's complex?

Yes, indeed, the world is badly made… Let's affirm this, at least, from time to time. Clear ideas, confusing feelings.

He who looks at a flower and thinks «brevity», is wicked.

Men seem more human when there is a trifle of degradation in our lives.

The mirror accuses you: look at yourself closely and you will realize it is so.

If you hide something, you are alive.

One needs a strong will power to not become an assasin.

Love lets us be stupid with impunity.

Deception… Is it worth it?

Wrath is also an opinion.

Any of your flaws will always be a lesser evil. Danger is attractive because it breaks one's routine.

Sometimes, abnegation is a form of irony.

Only self-respect prevents us from being envious.

Vicious people can never be satiated. And who does not have their own vices?

We have not learned it; we have been taught it!

To be compassionate is irritating.

And there always comes a time when love is a barely-veiled form of compassion.

Meditation in front of a fountain.— to drink without thirst: that would be more human.

We believe what is convenient for us to believe. No one is naive in this valley of tears.

There is only one bloodless way of living: sleeping.

Not nakedness, being dressed is indecent. But we are already accustomed to it, and in addition, the climate permits nothing more.

«Bad advice» is usually useless. Only those who do not need it pay attention to us.

We say something «is repulsive», but the truth is that we are afraid.

When a stupid person speaks, the air is contaminated.

People are them.

In the end, death does not only consist of dying. It is to die and to be forgotten. Sooner or later, forgotten.

It seems that fasting excites the imagination. But perhaps satiety will be even more exciting.

At some critical level, to believe in God is an impressive audacity. We must recognize its merit, if nothing else.

They have coffee, they drink brandy… Then, why are they against pornography?

Irony needs accomplices.

It is fine that you have renounced these «honors». But it was already dubious that you had deserved them.

To see things for what they are, predisposes some people to abhorring them.

«Guests and small fish, after three days they all stink», people say. Upon close inspection, everything stinks after three days: guests, small fish, pure poetry, quantum physics, buddhism, and you yourself.

Morality is more about ideas than about behavior.

    There are very evil ways of doing good.

Depending on the circumstances, poor appetite can ultimately seem like an abstinence or a sacrifice.

And are we not all apocryphal characters?

Personal Experience

It is not that I enjoy saying «I»; it is that I do not have the right to speak with a different personal pronoun.

I am an optimist: I close my eyes.

My contradictions are my hopes.

«En enfer je recevrai des coups de bec de toutes les perdrix que j'ai tuées» (J. Renard)[33]. So will I. But I won't regret it.

It does not matter if they lie to me. What really pisses me off is knowing that they are lying.

He who puts up with me loves me. There is no other explanation.

I shall die, I shall die, I shall die...What a pity (especially for me)! To die must be to stop writing.

It is when I am alone that I can think of others.

The most interesting part of my ideas (let's call them «mine») are the objections I could pose to them myself.

All forgetfulness is an amputation, and I am not conscious of it.

There are times when I think the clock is unjust.

I—so it seems to me—am Jewish. Are you not?

From a certain age on, I consider myself fortunate if my teeth are not hurting.

Ah, if only I could jettison my indignations!

I try to identify where my ignorance lies.

---

[33] "In Hell I will be pecked out by every partridge I have killed."

As for me, I am content with being *a little «right» from time to time*. To aspire for more seems bold to me.

I am afraid and I scream; I am afraid and I keep quiet. They are one and the same: I am afraid.

I live—so to speak—*quia absurdum*[34].

Because I do not dare say what I think, I strive to say what I should think.

Who can really know all his aversions?

We are born, and others rejoice; we die, and others mourn us. I cannot entirely understand it…

I am my superstition: the superstition of myself.

They hate me, and it does not matter; but they oblige me to hate them, and the latter does.

I imagine myself as others see me, and I pity myself slightly. But if I think about them, I realize it's not that bad.

The weak ones are *condemned* to be disloyal, liars, envious and astute. So, do not reproach them for it!

He (to me): —I share your opinions.

I: —I also share them, obviously. But only to a certain degree…

My adversary is my collaborator. *Malgré lui*[35], obviously.

You accuse me of being sarcastic. Why shouldn't I be? I can barely tolerate myself!

Everything I think and write at this moment, has been thought and written by several, if not countless people before me. If it were not so, it would be meritless.

I am perpetually convalescing from my prejudices.

I dislike intransigence because it is contagious.

The worst part of being old is that from the start, everyone intends to respect you.

Do they object to you? Then you have a chance of being right.

---

34 "Because it is absurd". A play on words with Tertullian´s famous saying, "I believe because it is absurd."
35 "Despite himself".

Ultimately, we always end up loving the shape of a nose.

They buy and sell: I do not belong to myself.

It is as pity, but we often lack the memories we want.

There are parts of nature that seem unfinished to me.

We all go through moments when we would like to be real idiots.

It is sad not to have had a relentless critic when we needed one the most.

When you are over forty, your desperations begin to seem comical to you.

Only the rich have an immortal soul.

Socrates, Mayakovsky, Pavese? The suicides that give us goosebumps are those of illiterate people.

I spy on myself and hence I sometimes realize what I'm doing.

I am thinking of you: couldn't you be a simple optic illusion? Love letters are always sad.

We usually say despondently: «He talks to himself». But everybody talks to themselves when they lack an interlocutor.

I am probably wrong. In any event, I must take that risk.

To be myself is unjust.

Like in the period of Julien Sorel— «Everybody should be be dismissed», and «there are no pleasures left apart from reading and agriculture » (*Le Rouge et le Noir*, I, ch. VII).

When I do not find an opponent, I try to imagine one.

Do not dwell on it: you are anthropomorphic by chance.

Behind every written or uttered word, so many unnecessary fermentations!

At dawn, all birds sing the same, just like at night all cows are black.

It is very hard to attain certainty, and even then it is always temporary.

«Piangerò la sorte mia[36]...». But in verse or with opera music.

---

36 "I shall lament my fate", title of an aria from Handel´s opera *Giulio Cesare in Egitto*.

My posterity will be made of paper.

Perhaps we are not happy with our face, but any portrait of us makes us happy.

A poet told me:

—A sudden toothache can frustrate a masterpiece.

Amongst all peoples, there are still some followers of Nietzche, late or instinctive. I have never known someone who affirmed:

—Piety is god's vice... But that tended towards sarcasm.

«Guilt»! What a word!

They say: «You are what you do». And they are right: «I am what I produce». With the well-known «capital gain» *y compris*.

Fire, it is so fast!!

The idea of «reciprocity» is astutely selfish. And in addition it explains the existence of «good samaritans».

Every day we find neophytes of something.

What do I know about you? What do I know about myself?

I do not ignore why, but in practice stallions don't seem indecent, and large families enjoy numerous considerations.

If only there were a devil with whom we could sign a deal!

Everybody is somebody else's subaltern.

I have confidence in the letter. Any written word, either *per se*, or *a contrario sensu*, is always revolutionary in the end. Everything consists of knowing how to choose.

Freedom and neuralgia are incompatible.

Be that as it may, logic is a consoling resource.

You can confirm it: the *allegro* of Vivaldi's concert number 1, opus 12 for violin and orchestra can be danced as a foxtrot.

We live furtively. Why?

Prey is an unacceptable concept for a skeptic. From time to time, the alternative is: either find it or retreat.

Philosophy and Letters

Literature consists of talking about literature.

To think is to deform. Like painting or writing poetry, but in a different way.

Pedagogy.— To know is knowing to repeat. I watch a painting and I see what I want.

Thank God Hegel is so hard to read. Otherwise, today, everybody would be a Hegelian.

Cello sounds like a sexton—at least like a precentor.

People do not blaspheme as much as before. If I were a monotheist, I would start worrying.

The dislikes of poets are feminine.

An honest intellectual begins by writing a sentence. The rest of his work will just be a process of rectifying what he wrote the first day.

Precision is also an art.

In reality, regarding respect for philosophy, only philosophers have it, and not all of them.

To a certain degree, all paintings are a self-portrait.

Originality.— Among all of us, we think everything.

Reading Kafka is a pleasureless masturbation.

And who are our neighbors? Jesus Christ stated: every person from whom we can receive some benefit. In fact, I do not know if Jesus Christ «stated» this, but that is what St Vincent Ferrer claims (*Sermons*, II, 91). On the other hand, the definition is beautiful.

When the painter paints, the world grows.

The artist is never obliged to justify his work. In principle, he is always right.

Perfection tends to lead towards mediocrity. Nevertheless, we should tend to perfection. Probably, the secret lies in stopping half-way.

The best human creation is the equilateral triangle.

«Le Philosophe sans le savoir»[37]. In some ways, the only one worthy of excuse.

Poetry is only good for more poetry.

Why did Archimedes, Pythagoras or Euclid not invent the biclycle?

Because of laziness or displicency?

T. S. Eliot was Queen Victoria's grandson.

Erudites are never detested, and that is the only explanation of the luxuriance of the historical sciences.

A statue is a ghost. Sculptors and spiritists will deny it, but it is so.

Hamlet… Buffalo Bill grafted onto Hamlet would be a really interesting type.

To amend and to augment: that is culture.

Nobody imitates in good faith.

Topic for a doctoral dissertation.— To determine the moment when Robinson Crusoe began *again* to feel the need for a philosophy.

To paint «from life»? When he is holding his paintbrushes, the painter must only watch the painting he is making.

Mr. Puigblanch, from Mataró, wrote: «Como estos pecados nacen de un excesivo amor a la propagación de la especie…» (*Opúsculos*, II, additions). Because these sins are born out of an excessive love for the propagation of the species…

All ideas end up suffering from rheumatism.

Curvy young ladies, like the earth and the sky, *enarrant gloriam Dei*[38]. That could be, if you wish, a senile opinion: it is, also, a good apologetic argument. I do not know why theologians have not exploited it.

A good book is always a provocation.

Someone will invent the art of supplementing truth's defects.

When we have decided that killing a tiger, a chicken, or a flea is not the same as killing a man, we have become human.

---

37 "The philosopher without knowing it". It is the title of a play by Michel-Jean Sedain.
38 "Are a manifestation of God's glory".

But that does not occur every day.

Dodecaphonic music is too foggy.

They say the value of gold is conventional; so is that of Balzac.

We must secularize the idea of abjection, just like in some countries cemeteries have been secularized.

Reading is easy, but how costly is writing?

Perhaps, contrary to the clàssic author, art is short, and life is, if not long, relatively long.

Health, good health, preserves you from philosophies. Hygiene, for instance, is «antimetaphysical»: at least functionally antimetaphysical.

Apostasy is outdated. Nowadays, it is only practiced by princes and princesses of marrying age, and even exclusively as a state matter.

To write is to remember, or in any case, to fabricate memories.

Only what is evident is reasonable. Reason, for the most part, depends on «sight».[39]

History of painting.— *Non saturatur oculus visu*[40] (*Ecc.*, I, 8).

Sex for the rich is more pathetic than sex for the poor. This is proven by Petrarch, Shakespeare, Corneille, Dumas Jr., Proust, Law- rence…

It is too late to preach hedonism.

In the western world, all grammars would be unthinkable if they did not have Aristotle's logic as their foundation.

In art, the most just form of realism is caricature.

How fortunate that Goya did not know how to paint! Otherwise, poor Charles IV's family!

Neanderthals, what was their idea of «human dignity»?

There are also intellectual astigmatisms, and one must recognize that they have greatly contributed to the prosperity of culture.

---

[39] The original *vista* refers both to 'sight' and to '(point of) view'.
[40] "The eye is not satisfied by seeing".

Stendhal.— It is enough that the «details» are «exact» (*voici des détails exacts*). The rest does not matter.

The truth is always a mystification of the truth.

(Possible) definition of philosophy— The art of grabbing the cow by its balls.

For more than a millenium, Western culture has been made by priests and the priests' students. We cannot do away with it from one day to the next.

Impressionism is «passing the time» painting.

The danger of «mastering a profession» is that art simply follows a «profession».

«Ce qui est noir n'est peut-être qu'obscur[41]...». Wake up. Colors and words do not have very clear boundaries.

Lot's wife turned her face, not out of curiosity, but rather out of malice.

I have read excellent criticisms *against* the venerable institution that is Syllogism. But they were also made through syllogisms.

The sound of the 17th and 18th century musicians has an advantage: it is soothing. Like symmetry.

Dictionary jewels.— «*Filosop (phil-, filosof)*..., 2, sick person's chamber pot» (*Diccionari Aguiló*, vol. IV, pàg. 57).

Mathematicians are a group of fraudulent poets, who, in fact, attempt to write the only poetry possible.

In art, memory is a mistake.

El Greco's characters, couldn't they be syphilitic?

Any premeditated noise can already be considered music.

Dialectical or not—for now, it is secondary—materialism. As far as philosophy is concerned, it does not even resemble a philosophy. What else can we ask for?

Only archaeologists know what time is.

---

41 "Black can't be but obscure".

The Art of Giving Rabbits[42]

Do not make your ignorance into an argument.

You need a rival to assert yourself. Don't destroy him! Take care of him, support him if necessary!

Be discreet: distracted, precisely.

If you do not retaliate, do it out of disdain.

Let your intentions be good always. They could serve you as an alibi.

Avoid excessive gratitude: it is usually sincere and, accordingly, annoying.

Make comparisons, and you'll begin to understand.

Do not demand clemency. If it is granted to you, you are being deceived. You have a body: use it, take advantage of it!

You think *this*. You believe you think *this*—what follows… Well. Try to re-think it. Re-think it. You'll see how, indeed, you were thinking *differently*.

We must be scrupulous: especially when choosing our scruples. Love, but not too much.

Do not spare any effort to go through open doors. If you do not pass through them, they will close them again.

The more friends you have, the more you will be able to lose.

Do not write verses on death: it is useless. Write your testament, which is more practical.

Tell the truth. That way you will take revenge.

If you listen when they talk, you will end up talking as well. It is a warning.

Amphitruo invites you for dinner. Say: Long live Amphitruo!

An enmity is not complete if it is not receiprocated. Whenever you find a candidate to be your enemy, do not let him get away.

Be courteous: believe what your wife tells you.

---

42 As indicated before, the original suggests an absurd play on words between two phonetically similar words, '(to give) advice' and '(to give) rabbits'.

Never stop protesting: something will always remain.

No, do not pay attention to those who talk about the loftiness—moral, of course—of pain, and go find a pain killer quickly.

We must trust chance. Not much, but some.

It is not enough to have a mattress at home. We must use it to be born, to sleep, to fornicate, and to die.

With some luck, you will end up believing that you are you.

If you have a son, teach him to be free. Even at your own detriment. In reality, it will have to be at your own detriment…

Those who doubt, do so because they can, not because they want to. Strive to doubt, however.

Concede when asked to do so. But try not to be asked.

Do not have more convictions than strictly necessary.

If you cannot falla sleep, try writing poetry. I am sure many great poets started this way.

Do not be insolent. They will think you are sincere!

Do not ask, for you will be answered, and who knows what.

It is very pleasant to be asked for something; Even more so to deny it.

Beware! Try to administer your ungratefulness well!

If you were to cry— literally or metaphorically—, do so with premeditation.

To foresee your friends: that is the secret.

When you refuse to talk about this or that, your refusal speaks for you.

And you? Are you not«bad company»?

Define yourself, if you so wish. But don't lose sight of the fact that to define onself is to expose one's private parts.

Bribe yourself, before somebody else does.

It is bad when your opinions are a consequence of your passions; even worse, when your passions are a consequence of your opinions.

Do not abstain yourself, now that you still can.

Let yourself be convinced by this, then, if you so wish. Provided, however, that you are equally disposed to let yourself be convinced by whatever follows.

At the expense of whom? Ask yourself that, from time to time.

Monotony also has its charm, and in addition, it is respectable.

«Advice» is a literary genre in decline: do not attempt to practice it.

Persevere and you will end up falling asleep.

First, we must know what is irreparable; then, we must accept it.

If you do not have money, let it go.

Hide, and if they find you, be it by chance.

In our private writings, which nobody must read, we must strive to make no gramatical mistakes.

When applicable, use smugness to hide your stupidity.

Let others make assertions; in the meantime, prepare a rebuttal.

In the age of cibernetics, what matters is knowing how to turn off a Machine.

Only humble people do not feel humiliated. You must not be humble.

Choose what is most convenient for you, but do not try to explain it to yourself.

Do not accept defeat until you stand to gain from it.

Someone looks you in the eye and you are disconcerted. But he likewise feels stared at, and he is not any less uneasy.

To be reasonable is to be vigilant.

If you wish to be loved by others, pretend to be like them, but better or worse

Did you say a *happening?* I would love to see it, improvised at the door of a factory.

Be foresighted: make sure your shroud fits you.

You are your own neurosis. But at the first opportunity you have, go to a psychiatrist.

I exhort you to go horseback riding. In the future classless society, you will not have the opportunity. Not now either, it is true. Nevertheless, I exhort you. It is pleasant.

We must have a seat, anywhere possible.

You must read Henry Miller because the truth is you would not endure Rabelais any more. And in the end, with one or the other, you will run into the endless and enlightening epic of the zipper fly.

What are you doing now? That is *already* a senile passion!

If you insist, do so in bad faith.

They treat you as if you were a thing. Because you are a thing, quantifiable and appraisable. Your duty is to know this.

Five bodily senses! Let us demand more of them!

Tomorrow will be another day and I could care less. Let us start from the beginning then.

Since you want to receive compensation, wake up: you do not have any right to it and must fabricate it.

A well-played violin, a barbiturate, a dose of alcohol…

Do not pander to yourself: it is no fun.

«All is happy…».[43] He who is not content is so out of his own volition. Like in the children's game: «Shut your eyes and open your hand…».

They Call It «SOCIETY»

Idleness, in the end, is nothing more than an ideology.

The invention of cloth was one of the first episodes of class struggle.

No one can demand serenity from their victim.

When fear is not innocent, then it is not fear, it is cowardice.

I have a bit of freedom, and I think to myself: who is paying for me?

You eat, you chew: practically, with a mouthfull, you are muzzled.

---

43 With the meaning 'all is well'. The original states 'nothing is unhappy, sad'.

The sexual income *per capita*! That should also be indicated by statistics!

«Saintes baïonnettes de France[44]...» (Michelet). All wars would like to be wars of religion.

The one in charge wants his subordinates to be docile. Every philosophy of history must stem from this platitude.

Shout to see if they make us be quiet.

«In the sage's house, wealth is enslaved; in the ignoramus's house, it is the master». So said Seneca. Who was, obviously, wealthy.

Racism.— Blacks are not the same as whites because they are black.

Only premature revolutions are redoubtable, because they end badly.

«Because he is speaking in Catalan...let us see what he said». The decasyllable is equally correct, and its content, more reasonable.

The myth does not claim that Prometheus is dead. It would behoove us to remember this.

«Les capacités de la bourgeoisie s'en vont...». The capacities of the bourgeoisie disappear, indeed, does not know how to be leftist anymore.

There are intrepid women; they even enjoy having grandchildren.

The aspiration to abolish private property meets a difficult obstacle: the prehensile capacity of hands.

Is whoever pays in charge? History and daily experience show, at least, that those in command are reimbursed. To command is to be reimbursed—among other things.

Frederick the Great, at the very least, had the merit of knowing how to compose music over Hitler or De Gaulle.

The defeated fall quickly out of fashion.

Perhaps work dignifies men. I am not sure. But it certainly tires them.

In a so-called «consumer society» it does not rain, nor snow, nor is it sunny.

---

44 "Holy French bayonetes".

Someone has said that kepis deform the head. But not only kepis, also topees, skullcaps, top hats, berets, judge's caps—not to mention Catalan caps!.

Before judges, surveyors was created. The latter are a premise of the former.

The eve of war, usually, or almost always, seems like a festivity.

Conservative people like to obey, which is why they are conservative.

They fight against spermatozoa as if they were Koch's bacillus.

There are rulers for whom to govern is a matter of revenge.

Who assured that «it is not possible to be above using bayonets»? No, no. There are asses capable of anything.

Sometimes, bloodstains are decorative. Read Plutarch.

«La liberté consiste à ne dépendre que des lois[45]...». How candid, how very candid this Voltaire! As if laws were not made by them!

One becomes rich the moment one fears becoming poorer than one already is.

Lenin, or Marx, or both, say that up until now all revolutions have ultimately reinforced the governmental machine. As well as their reactions. The governmental machine is continuously reinforced by any excuse.

The Sardana dance is «republican» and «federal», as Eugeni d'Ors pointed out. Perhaps because of this it is in decline.

«All power comes from God». But the powerful, where do they come from?

The enemies of equality, of egalitarianism, are so, among other loftier reasons, out of fear of recognizing they are too «equal».

Dictatorship intoxicates.

The condemnation of selfishness, when does it not occur in the name of other selfishness? (Parallel: The condemnation of nationalism, when does it not..., etc.?)

To be conservative is very easy: it is enough to forget that one can be conservative without realizing it.

---

45 "Freedom depends on depending on laws".

Any idea, or ideology, is good enough to justify a crime, and history is full of such cases. The evil part, naturally, does not lie in the crime, but rather in its justification.

Genesis, 3:19.— But because sweat can evaporate…

They make war because of their profession, they torture because of their profession, they deceive because of their profession… Aren't they able to make a living differently?

Democracy is uncertain. That is why everyone fears it.

«Du pouvoir absolu vous ignorez l'ivresse[46]», proclaimed one of Racine's characters. Or as they claim someone said: «To be in command is so pleasant!».

Our vocabulary is tainted by classism. We talk about «noble taste», and a dog «without his owner» is called «an abandoned dog», and not a «free dog».

The only advante of being ordered is that you are not ordering.

Wars, they should be waged by the elderly. They would be less biologically onerous.

In addition, wars are always declared by old people.

Crowds revolt or obey, but they do not reason. There lies the problem. We must be hopeful…

Any power is an abuse of power. That goes with the very nature of things.

What Republic would not give in to the temptation of having a Bonapart defending it?

Freedom is a habit, and it's not very easy to acquire.

It can only be acquired through practice!

I have been able to observe that conservative people, when it rains, are even more conservative.

Ethnography and folklore.— Men were terrified by silence, and they invented the drum. Then, with the drum, they made warfare and dances.

Nowadays, a revolution cannot not be sacrilegious.

---

46 "You ignore how much absolute power intoxicates".

Your political adversary will accuse you of not doing what you should have done, or of doing it, if you did do it. That is part of the game.

Without anthems, without banners, without victories.

They say tyrannies always end badly. Perhaps. But *que les quiten lo bailao!*[47]

Regicide has fallen out of fashion. Kennedy's case was an anachronism.

We should not get tired of repeating it: all freedoms are solidary.

If you look at it from the outside, you will find that in every «system», heresy is more frightening than orthodoxy.

As things stand today, to be Catalan is just a mere hypothesis.

«Non-intervention in the domestic matters of another country».— Bofill i Mates (*L'altra concòrdia*, pàg. 50) Defined it as such: «To mutually grant themselves, each sovereign power, carte blanche to freely oppress their subjects».

Who knows why, but the poor usually vote for conservative candidates.

And so do the rich, of course.

Painting has, when compared to literature, the disadvantage of not being able to be immoral, or of being so only when the paint is no longer authentic.

Power exudes a patrimonial concept of power: the one in charge is the master.

We breath as they did during the Paleolithic. We haven't advanced at all, in this aspect.

A dog is more valuable alive than a lion is dead? It depends how and for what!

How is discipline kept.— Philippe Pétain said it, and did it (June 12, 1917): «Une première impression de terreur est indispensable, et c'est aux premiers exemples qu'est due l'amélioration constatée[48]...» (Gilbert Guilleminault, *La France de la Madelon*, pag. 159).

In the last hour, the Capitol is saved by any geese.

---

47 "They can't take the fun he has had away from him".
48 "A first impression of terror is essential, and it is to the first examples that the improvement observed is due."

I Am Temporarily Closing the Parenthesis

Debatable affirmations and denials, I admit. Perhaps they will be useful precisely because of this, because they are debatable: because they prompt discussion.

Few Words

These notes, brief and sometimes epigrammatic, are a continuation of the book Consells, proverbis i insolències[49] *that I published in 1968. I have many more in the drawer. I have not made a hasty selection, and I would not want anybody to interpret this one as particularly significant. To write an aphorism is usually a slow process, costly in rectifications, perplex in ratifications, responsible for the nuances of some word or other. It is an archaic and not very fashionable «literary genre», although they fascinate me. They are one more «paper hat», which only aspires to have the interest of a personal «point of view» in mind. Contradictory? Perhaps, perhaps not. And I do not care.*

We are human because we have been raised amongst humans, and more or less, we have learned to be one.

The one consolation about being mortal is that others are just as mortal, or even more.

Decadence of «cynicism».— Before, from time to time, in small villages, you could see dogs mating on the streets.

Fear is always voluntary.

Orthodoxies, «systems», sooner or later, end up producing a bitter feeling of claustrophobia.

There is this sadness, or melancholy, produced by knowing that we will never know *everything*.

One Jew for another, between Spinoza and Kafka, I choose Spinoza.

When you begin a conversation with someone, in fact, you are already asking them for a favor.

A love that lasts a long time needs another name.

You do not need to be ungrateful. To be sincere is enough.

---

49 As indicated by Salvador in the prologue to this translation, "the title of the volume puts together semantically three types of verbal activities: advising, stating expressions coined as popular wisdom, and daring, nerve or even insult".

Modern philosophy is dialectal. «Cogito, ergo sum[50]». «Sum», what does it mean: I am, I exist? Ah!

No one has «original» ideas; at best, one has «fixed» ideas. In general, an obstinacy can also become an argument.

Envy is usually very clairvoyant.

The only reprehensible thing about suicide is that it almost always involves a premature death. And, on closer inspection, is there any death that is really premature? Everybody dies rather late.

Beware of friends that can become enemies. They know how you are already.

«Error also has merit», said Voltaire. And if he was mistaken in saying it, he was only stating something evident.

We are all slightly impostors: for instance, when we say «I». Do not trust your *conscience*. It will tend to agree with you.

What or who am I? Alain said: «Cette unité logique de moi même[51]...». Perhaps so. But provided it includes rheumatism, the Oedipus complex, the orgasm…

To read Vergil today, or Shakespeare, or even Proust or Miller, isn't it an anachronism?

«Corruption of minors»? A minor is probably not an adult until he is properly «corrupted».

Do not forget nor forgive injuries. Simply pretend you had never received them.

Let there be no misunderstanding: The fulfillment of freedom is licentiousness. Allow me to say in passing, that I concur.

If Wittgenstein does not serve to «abolish» philosophy, what was Wittgenstein good for then?

When I say «no», am I not saying «yes»?

Memories.— One day—the only day I talked about these things—, Don Vicent Alfaro pointed out to me that: «If you consider it carefully, Blasco Ibáñez, in his novels, has never portrayed a Valencian character as anything short of a son of a bitch...». Indeed, a topic for a doctoral dissertation.

---

50 "I think, therefore I am."
51 "This logical unity of myself".

A word for each thing? Dictionaries would never end. There are so many «things» that are not even things!

One way of taking revenge on the world is to make children.

To talk is already to exaggerate.

Perfection is also an act of mercy.

You cannot be persuasive without some perfidy.

History of art.— What Michelangelo knew how to paint and sculpt were chicken and eggs. His female breasts, for instance, are a real disgrace.

It is not worth it to be proud: it is very tiring, at that.

What are they saying? It does not matter! Object to it. At least you will have fun.

This is the conclusion I have reached: there is only one «mortal sin», and that is to make gramatical errors.

«Be who you are», said some classic author, which humanists have parroted as a motto. Well. Try it. In any event, we cannot be anything else.

Life—and not only human life—is, so to speak, a big theological evil. Those who want to will understand.

To be stoic is a good thing. But only sometimes, and, if possible, from time to time.

Hypocrisy was invented, was it not? Then you would be mistaken in not taking advantage of it.

Have you seen anything more mysterious than a finger? Or than a fingernail.

All deities have been invented to fuck with human beings. And it is man who has invented them. From the Paleolithic forward, paranoia is the «human condition». Karl Marx was no exception to the rule.

Ecology.— And the thousands, or millions and millions of animal and vegetable species that went extinct before the first industrial smog?

Neurasthenias, well administered, have always yielded good results. Lyric poetry, for instance.

I have the right to be how I am, for no other reason than that I was born this way. And this is the problem, if you're intention is the same.

Music is a conspiracy against silence, be it Bach or rock. But, has silence ever existed?

«He knows more than God…». This popular expression is not a blasphemy: it is a comparison, a reference to absolute magnitudes…

The rose, without the literature that it has abundantly recieve, would just be a tiny cabbage, tasteless and deceptively colored. Its aroma, in the kitchen, would fade away. Josep Pla was mistaken.

Everything is uncertain. Let's imagine, for instance, that every morning, when shaving, we look at ourselves in the mirror. Or the ladies putting on their makeup. Who is who?

«Con tu ausencia y veinte reales / un duro mi pecho gana». And some even dare say that Campoamor was not a great poet!

Against boileau.— Before thinking, learn how to write.

First, listen to it; then, do not believe it; finally, forget it.

There are definitions that offend. Or perhaps I should say that some definitions are deliberately offensive.

Every time we talk, we talk in «self defense».

To be mortal is not worth it. That's why we realize it too late.

Have I been able to graciously hide my misanthropy? In any event, it was a literary obligation.

We should not be too reminiscent. Memory, frequently, is resentful.

If you do not Hunt the hare, there will be no hare stew. To make trout, you must cut the eggs. Where there is no blood, there is no sausages. Ectcetera. You have been warned.

Escape or hide: Even better: escape and hide. If you can, of course.

We feel a strange voluptuosity by discovering the fact that our adversary is stupid. Nonetheless, this solves nothing.

Every cynicism is based, essentially, on mistrust.

Strive to love. Belated love is not love: it is a mania.

I dislike being outraged. But if I am not outraged from time to time, what would be of me?

Since being reasonable is not mandatory, people take advantage of it.

In the end, all tombs are desecrated.

We are so vulnerable, the idea itself can kill us.

Develop the passion you find most pleasant, but make it temporary, or at least intermittent.

With what is freedom incompatible?

There are days in which some sound, just a sliver of sound, makes you happy.

To be ingenious and to be right—which is the case with Gibbon, Johnson, Voltaire, Wilde, according to Borges— usually seems monstruous. And it actually is something monstruous. On the other hand, we are fascinated by monsters.

Terror also has its *voyeurs*.

Why should we be ecclectic for no reason?

Making love solves nothing, but it helps pass the time.

The fate of those who write, like me, is to become illegible, some day, or even right now.

I do not know why we refer to someone—about anyone at all—as having «bad intentions». They simply have their own intentions. The problem with «good intentions» is different.

Between good and evil, both of an afflictive nature, we could aspire to happiness.

These observations are nothing special. They are just «particular» insofar as I make them my own.

Look at it this way: the fact that they don't say anything about you is, frequently, a lie, and sometimes, even slander.

Every morning—regarding color, sounds, ideas—demands its own word, and dictionaries are not so generous.

Serenity can also be achieved through obstinacy.

Anthropocentrism.— From a human standpoint, man is rather sordid.

Undoubtedly, the wolf does not hate the sheep when he devours it. Be that as it may, he devours it.

Whenever you breathe, you incur the responsibility of breathing.

Everything can be an object of devotion. There are more saints than chapels.

Alphabetical order is just a variety of public order.

The entomologist observes his collection of dissected butterflies and finds self-justification: «In the end, they were going to die».

All societies consider sloth as a sort of sabotage.

There are no sacrileges; just simple profanities.

The only respectable ideal is satiety. Well: the sum of all satieties.

An excess of tolerance would terminate any civilization, and all «ci- vilitzations» are very conscious of this.

They take a picture of you, you look at it and think: «Luckily it is temporary! How reckless of me to allow them to take my picture!».

It is good to have a «patria», be it natural, adopted or military: everybody manages the best they can. But «patriotism», isn't it a hypertrophy?

New perplexities! Come on, come on!

Nowadays, a plane falls, cars crash, there are domestic disputes, and there are quite a few casualties: newspaper headlines refer to them as «tragedies». Not at all! «Tragedies are so called because they include tearful stories about the cruelties of kings or great princes…». Antigone was Antigone, and Oedipus was Oedipus, and Shakespeare's ghosts wore crowns. Vocabulary deteriorates.

We should not resign ourselves to the term «conscientious objectors». «objectors of unconsciousness» would be equally valid. We should encourage «objections».

To say «I» is redundant.

To be old and smile is nothing but treason.

It is unacceptable to be yourself.

Let us be humble: if it rains or shines tomorrow, it is not up to us.

The French Revolution, in the long run, has also served to establish compulsory military service. In fact, «serving» is the theme.

It is a pity to be tall when others are of short stature.

Against a «fait accompli» there is no answer save another «fait accompli». That is: a «provocation» provokes more «provocations». Everything depends on whether it is advantageous for them or not.

Reading—adapted—of Isiah 44:6: «I am the first, and I am the last; and there is no I besides myself». The label is secondary.

Knees, as well as elbows, are decisive. More so in politics than in athletics. Also in literature.

One day the world will end, and everything will be irrelevant.

You always say the same things. Truly, that is what is expected of you.

To play with fire is exciting, undoubtedly. Any danger has the allure of surprise.

The turtle has not stopped being a philosophical animal. Look at it.

Nature, obviously, does not create gardens. Is there anything more artificial than a garden?

All theories have a possible refutation: refusal. Te refute is to refuse, with a curious etymological coincidence.

Since doctors do not prescribe it, people do not «think».

Testimonies are «false testimonies» from the moment someone believes in them.

If you get distracted, you will say something else.

It is very sad to have to feel sad.

The more ambiguous words are, the more they facilitate coexistence.

There are those who think that the Lord Our God entertained himself modeling Adam's fingers so that, centuries later, Mozart could play the piano.

Do not be deceived: to say «good morning» is already writing literature

There must be many ways of commanding, I suppose. There is only one way to obey, and that is with humility. We can ruminate on this while waiting, patiently, at a traffic light.

«I am right», «you are right», «to concede»... How proper!

About Other Final Judgments

I

[Published in *La Nostra Revista*, num. 61 (Mexico, July 1951), pp. 342–343.]

When faith has been lost, one does not remain in a total religious neautrality. Either there is resentment or nostalgia. Sometimes there is a mixture of both: those are desperate cases.

Solitude is the only virile virtue. I mean: the only one women cannot practice and the only one that deserves to be practiced by men.

If there is anything intrinsically evil in this world, it is, without a doubt, the State.

There is an urgent need for a semantic readaptation of certain consecrated phrases. For instance, we should say: *He who is free of complexes, cast the first stone.* Or: *The sixth, suffer with patience your neighbour's neurosis.*

The Middle Ages could be democratic with impunity because they were not liberal. Nowadays, if God cannot solve it, we will stop being liberal because of democracy. (Note: by liberalism I understand anything except the mysticism of legality.)

An epigram for the diploma of students of medicine or theology.— You are invincible, oh Death; but we know you, and there lies our strength.

It is revealing: from the Middle Ages on, pilgrims no longer go to the Holy Land; they go to Rome, perhaps out of convenience.

Unamuno, what a scarcely sensual man! He never learned to find pleasure in music, nor the ocean, nor liturgy...

Perhaps the formula for anti-totalitarianism could be: *to govern with the opposition.* But one doubts its viability when considering that there is still a revolution pending.

Tolstoy: here you have the deplorable example of a moral without religion, when taken to its final consequences. Which are: denial, sterility, sadness.

I am sure that at their deepest core, most antisemites are such because Jews invented the feeling of sin and disseminated it throughout.

All vices are children of leisure, without excluding philosophy. If you have some free time and want to spend it, it is easy for you to engage in a dialogue like this:

—Where can we go?

—It does not matter. What matters is to find something to pass the afternoon.

—Careful! You do not have to pass the afternoon. The afternoon will have to pass through you.

—Or it will have to pass in you. Etc.

This *amateur* metaphysics, with a bit of skill, can become a respectable theory, or at least a rather pleasant imitation of *The Magic Mountain*.

II

[Published in *Pont Blau*, num. 3-4 (Mexico, November-December 1952), pp. 19-20.]

Josep Pla's opinions—let's call them ideas—are always trivial and vulgar. On the other hand, Pla is endowed with a sensorial capacity of extraordinary voracity. I vacillate between callin it sybarite or glutinous.

Regardless, it appears that it is not very frequent in any literature. This singles him out and saves him.

On Impressionism.— It is difficult to distinguish whether the painter, tempted by the light, chooses to paint landcapes, or if, on the contrary, obliged to paint landscapes by an imperative of Romantic influence, he does not find any other interesting plastic value than light.

Another impoverished word: *fable*. Is there anything more vulgar—less fabulous than those «animal stagings» of common sense?

It seems stupid: but the first requirement to be a cynic is that others do not follow suit.

«I'd rather be a Publican than a Pharisee!»—said once Mr. Josep Maria de Sucre.

«Here you have—I thought to myself—a subtle proposal from a Pharisee».

The baby, which was one of those who is well-behaved in principle, remained quiet, with his eyes wide open and his fists closed. The lady who was visiting had been noticing it for a long time. Finally she commented philosophically:

—Poor little ones! They must be so bored!

Poets are always *incomparable*. But incomparable also with regard to themselves.

Geometry has always been present in the square. A sort of skeleton. Endoskeleton (classical art, for instance) or exoskeleton (Cubism or abstract art, to name other examples). In all cases, a bone: a bone that we remove mechanically when we are about to «consume» a painting.

Requiem for André Gide.— Here you have a death before which there can only be silence, a thick, silence. No prayer, no elegy, no literary summary. It has been a simple, impassive death. It could even be said that it has been a resigned death: but this is a rather Christian word for this case. André Gide died as he lived: sincerely. In his most testing final days, he did not allow himself to be defeated by the great ghosts. He had always fought them. His old age was beatifully invulnerable.[52] And God,

Who does not adopt partial measures, will have received in His glorious memory the name of this great spirit. Of this religious and tenacious spirit. Because Gide was above all else a restless searcher of truths. Perhaps he only found one: *his*. (And is it possible to find any truth other than ours, to each their own, unyielding, precise?) Gide found *his* truth and strove to live it, to live in it loyally. At least he was able to express it. «Every one who does not express themselves— leaves in writing that they are useless and doleful». Gide expressed himself: in a clear and valiant manner. It is his greatest lesson—almost his only lesson. To review it, I have opened up one of his books, at random. Now is the moment to read him once more, as a respectful and staunch homage. That is what he would have wished. That is how the priest who presided over his funeral, at Cuverville, would have wished as well when he substituted the requiem with the pages of *Numquid et tu?* (February, 1951.)

Joanot Martorell was Ausiàs March's brother-in-law. In this case we can say that their *affinity* was strictly legal.

---

52 The phonetic similarity between 'vellesa' and 'bellament', 'old age' and 'beautifully', is lost in the English translation.

Urbanism.— The art of painting the helmet of traffic Police white.

I find those men pleasant who, like Bloy or Maurras nowadays, have been able to obtain so many, and such diverse and such complete animosities.

III

[Published in *Pont Blau*, num. 26 (Mexico, December 1954), pp. 420–421.]

Ors said about Maragall, with a certain tone of recrimination, that he was an *interjectional* poet. The term seems accurate to me, but not its appraisal. I believe a poet is a poet insofar as he is able to turn each word into an interjection. By interjectioning the language, he saves it from death and didactics.

«Balzac quotidien», as Le Corbusier said.— There are people that only read the events section in newspapers; even worse than these, perhaps, are those who do not read that section ever. The former delight with mere curiosity; the latter are obstinate in their ignorance. Nevertheless, both fail to see the pain that is most constant, most instructive, most sad, that life possesses. And above all, they forget that they themselves are vulnerable to be the protagonists of one of these headlines…

Julien Benda was (yes, in the past tense: was) not only an illustrious literary fossil but also the absolute opposite of what he wanted to be, that is, a burgeois, nationalist and politician. A threefold *traitor*.

What a *clerc*, man!

On the exceptionality of the writer— Certainly, man is a

«featherless biped[53]». But writers have at least one feather with which to write. Even if only metaphorically. That gives them a certain family resemblance to Indians and peacocks..

I would not know how to interpret it. But the fact is that, twenty or twenty-five years ago, only Surrealists still quoted Ramon Llull and recommended reading him. Afterwards, not even Surrealists.

---

53 As attributed to Plato by Diogenes Laertius.

With some ability and certain indifference, we can find a justification for everything. Why then waste time justifying anything? And nonetheless, we spend our lives justifying ourselves. You see: I am doing it myself while writing this…

IV

[Published in *Pont Blau*, num. 40 (Mexico, February 1956), pp. 54–55.]

Leonardo said that painting is «nature's niece». I am not saying that it was not, during his time. Nowadays, its relationship is more similar to that of mother-in-law and daughter-in-law.

Proparoxytones.— Metaphysics is an academic survival of nechromancy.

After Romanticism, Western literatures began to have a local smell—besides color and taste.

The French, a bedroom smell—from Paris or the provinces—with the whisperings of adultery.

The Spanish, of *cocido*[54], and poor *cocido*.

The German, of a mesocratic or university beerhouse, it depends. The Russian, of consumptive sweat.

The Italian, of *camerino*[55].

The English, of tea of sterile gentlemen.

The Catalan, of a shop, obviously; rather, of a small shop.

All this conforms to the prototypical stereotypes. What can we do! I—I swear, dear reader— am not at fault.

When politics requires sacrifices—«human sacrifices» or otherwise—, it has regretfully started to be confused with religion.

All this seems perfect to me: to end with the exploitation of man by man. But then, who will be the exploiter?

---

54 "Stew", humble food.
55 "Dressing room".

V

[Published in *Cap d'Any*, at Raixa, Palma de Mallorca, 1956.]

No, you shouldn't be nervous because of these things. What I just wrote, indeed, is very similar to what another gentleman has already written. It would not surprise me if the resemblance was almost literal. But I insist, your «originalitaty» should not be compromised because of it. That resemblance is, always, purely *coincidental*. And take heed: two people can only coincide in one place—or one idea—when they come from different directions. «Originality» lies, in the end, in the origin.

In any event, the plagiarist also plays his role. Naturally, in choosing appropriately what he plagiarizes.

Flere cum flentibus et gaudere cum gaudentibus. Sor Isabel de Villena translated it thus: «Plorar ab los qui ploren e alegrar-se ab los qui virtuosament se alegren[56]». Let us emphasive, then, the effusive point of view of the abbess:

I) that there exist non-virtuous happiness; II) that instead, crying—and pain, I suppose—is always virtuous. That verse from Dante.— How obvious! We can only be conscious of happiness—of *having been* happy—in the moment of misery. A man who knew he was happy would begin to not be so, he would no longer be happy.

When referring to private property, one typically says that it is an institution of natural law. And most proprietors interpret it to mean that what is naturally legal is Land Holding.

Il n'y a qu'une tristesse, c'est de n'être pas de Saints[57]. There must two, then. For we should also take into account the sadness of saints when they see those who are not.

Adam.— I cannot imagine laughter when men existed in an innocent state. Laughter, unprovoked by tickling, always implies malice.

Philosophers go out in search of the truth. At least, that is what they claim. But inevitably, their fate is like Columbus, who, as they say, on his way to the Indies happened upon America. The destiny of the philosophers—what can we do!—is to discover America: dazzling lands, perhaps extremely rich. When well

---

56 "To cry with those who are crying and to rejoice with those who rejoice". The Catalan adds "virtuously" to "rejoice".
57 "There exists only one sadness, that of not being saints" (Léon Bloy).

considered, it is nothing more than luck. Particularly, if we consider that the sought-after Indies are, surely, an inconsistent mythological reference.

Art, monsieur Gide said, «begins where *living* is not enough to explain life», that is, where there is an excess of life. And yes: it is incontrovertible that much art originates in the application of extravagant energy. But *also* there is art that is born to remedy a lack, a vital deficiency: to *compensate for it*. Perhaps the latter art is more abundant than the former.

It is obvious that, deep down, everything depends on what we understand by «life»…

In a dialogue, it is more important to listen to others than to talk.

There is no judgment without prejudice But the first prejudice must be the acceptance of others' prejudices. I know that this is impossible. Let us bemoan it. It is one of the biggest consequences of the original sin.

Aesthetically, naturalists were right in large part. Only that they were mistaken—by default—in what is understood by nature. «Moi, je suis aussi nature», Braque said.

VI

[Published in *El Pont*, num. 8.]

Chopin.— *O felix culpa*[58]!

A bad instint inclines us to believe that an *error*, that acutely frightening thing we call an *error*, is any way of thinking divergent from our own. That is why intolerance usually seems simultaneously dangerous and difficult.

We cannot forget the ingredient of caricature that is in the work of contemporary painters. Of tragic caricature, when considered carefully. Thanks to them, contemporary art always leaves us with a bitter aftertaste, with no other precedent in western history than perhaps the agonizing miracle of Bosch.

I am sure that the majority, not to say the entirety, of writers who have existed in the world since literature was invented, uncapable of deserving heaven or hell, will end up in Limbo. (Or perhaps they have never left it?)

* * *

---

58 "Oh blessed sin", part of the Easter Vigil.

CATALAN STUDIES
IN CULTURE AND LINGUISTICS
Edited by Antonio Cortijo Ocaña

Vol. 1 Antonio Cortijo Ocaña / Jordi M. Antolí Martínez (eds.): Approaches to New Trends in Research on Catalan Studies. Linguistics, Literature, Education and Cultural Studies. 2021.

Vol. 2 Marco Antonio Coronel Ramos (ed.): Mito y realidad: investigaciones sobre el pensamiento dual en el mundo occidental. 2022.

Vol. 3 Judit Freixa / M. Isabel Guardiola / Josep Martines / M. Amor Montané (eds.): Dictionarization of Catalan Neologisms. 2022.

Vol. 4 Adolf Piquer / Adéla Koťátková (eds.): Character and Gender in Contemporary Catalan Literature. 2022.

Vol. 5 Alejandro Llinares Planells / Guillermo López Juan (eds.): Rethinking Violence in Valencia and Catalonia. 2024.

Vol. 6 Joan de Déu Martines Llinares: Lèxic i Natura en les narracions d'Enric Valor. 2024.

Vol. 7 Hotel Paris Vicent Andrés Estellés Edition, Foreword and Translation by Dominic Keown. 2024.

Vol. 8 Forthcoming.

Vol. 9 Joan Fuster Aphorisms: Translated into English by Antonio Cortijo-Rodgers Studies by Antonio Cortijo-Rodgers and Vicent Salvador. 2024.

www.peterlang.com

www.ingramcontent.com/pod-product-compliance
Ingram Content Group UK Ltd.
Pitfield, Milton Keynes, MK11 3LW, UK
UKHW041449180426
11946UKWH00002B/18